WITHDRAWN

STATE & DISCRIMINATION
The Other Side of the Cold War

STATE & DISCRIMINATION
The Other Side of the Cold War

LYNN TURGEON

M. E. Sharpe, Inc.
ARMONK, NEW YORK
LONDON, ENGLAND

Available in the United Kingdom and Europe from M. E. Sharpe,
Publishers, 3 Henrietta Street, London WC2E 8LU.

Library of Congress Cataloging-in-Publication Data
Turgeon, Lynn. 1920–
    State and discrimination : the other side of the cold war /
Lynn Turgeon
        p.   cm.
    Bibliography: p.
    Includes index.
    ISBN 0-87332-532-X
    1. Discrimination—Economic aspects. 2. Economic history—
1945–   . 3. World politics—1945–   . I. Title. II. Title: Other side of
the cold war.
JC575.T87   1989
305—dc20   89-6437
                                                                    CIP

Printed in the United States of America
BB 10 9 8 7 6 5 4 3 2 1

Contents

Preface

The origins of this book can be traced back to the curriculum reforms in the late sixties and the development of "Black Studies" programs at major universities in the United States. Under the guidance of Hofstra's Dean of Liberal Arts, Joseph Astman, faculty were encouraged to develop an inter-disciplinary approach to the problems of minority groups.*

Twenty years of teaching a course entitled "Economics of Discrimination," which eventually attracted women as well as other minority students, is reflected in this book's contents and conclusions. The author is especially grateful to Dr. Murray Yanowitch, who team taught with him in the fall of 1969, when the course was receiving a trial run. As teachers of comparative economic systems, we both quite naturally encouraged our students to make international comparisons of the discrimination problem.

Travels throughout Eastern Europe the following summer convinced me that the greatest similarity between the problems of blacks in the United States and minority problems in Eastern

---

*For details on the development of this program at Hofstra University, see my "The Economics of Discrimination," monograph no. 62 of the Institute of World Economy (nee Center for Afro-Asian Research) of the Hungarian Academy of Sciences, Budapest, 1973 (also in Hungarian), especially pages 7 to 9. This is an expanded version of a talk given at the Petofi Club in Budapest in June, 1970.

Europe was to be found in the postwar condition of the remaining Gypsy (Rom) population, which still existed in Czechoslovakia, Romania, Bulgaria, and especially Hungary. In studying the Gypsy problem, the author is especially indebted to Dr. Milena Hubschmannova of Prague. In the fall of 1985, Hofstra University and IREX cooperated in facilitating fieldwork in Budapest, where the following persons contributed in various important ways: Istvan Dobozi, Eva Ehrlich, Gabor Revesz, Mihaly Simai, and especially Janos Timar.

Among the memorable students contributing to this course and indirectly to the contents of this book were: Bob Kirsch, Robert N. Horn (now Professor of Economics at James Madison University), Sharon Oster, (now Professor of Economics at Yale University), Morty Schapiro (now Professor of Economics at Williams College), and David Stewart.

Others who have read and commented critically on the manuscript (or parts thereof) at various stages of its development were: Tom Belmonte, Bettina Berch, Ednaldo Da Silva, Michael Ellman, Renee Ford, Ray Franklin, Jeff Frieden, Paula Garb, David Gleicher, Mark Glick, Morty Greenhouse, William Mandel, Robert McIntyre, Gottfried Paasche, Howard Sherman, David W. Southern, Howard Stanback, Alan Weiss, and Mike Wyzan. My indebtedness to all of the above in no way implicates them in its conclusions. Finally, special thanks to Susanna Sharpe, Manny Knight, Jim Merritt, and Scott Redhead for editorial assistance.

Introduction

State and Discrimination examines the political economy of the Cold War. Its thesis is that the competition between the two superpowers for world stature and public approval, particularly in the Third World, has forced each giant to pursue some policies that are antithetical to the solution of contemporary stabilization and growth problems of the respective economic systems.

For the United States, competition with the USSR has forced a change in the state's racial policies and general treatment of minorities, as foreseen by Gunnar Myrdal's *An American Dilemma*. Although women constitute a majority of our population, they have all of the economic characteristics of a minority group and have thus also benefited somewhat as free riders from the competitive coexistence of the behemoths. Figuratively speaking, blacks have been opening the doors that women have been walking through.

For the USSR, competition with the United States has accelerated the implementation of environmental policies that might well have been delayed until a more propitious time period. And this competitive struggle has forced Soviet planning authorities to imitate or react to United States military developments, albeit after some delay, as a result of breakthroughs in United States defense and offense technology.

Thomas Sowell and the University of Chicago "no free lunch" school have emphasized the historic volatility of our government's policy with respect to minorities.[1] The present book makes a case for a great reduction, if not the elimination, of this volatility after 1948. Soviet ideology and the future of East-West relations being what they are, the long-term prospects for minorities, including women, appear to be somewhat brighter in both countries as a result of their competitive coexistence.

Mainstream economists have traditionally assumed that greater "efficiency" is a legitimate objective of economic policy at both macroeconomic (the economy as a whole) and microeconomic (firm or household unit) levels. Thus, the role of government is to be generally minimized relative to the efficiency-producing free market forces which supposedly prevail outside the government sector. If government activity is to be justified, it must pass some sort of cost-benefit test: the social benefits of government activity must exceed their social costs. At the microeconomic level, the firm or enterprise is guided by profit-maximizing principles, assuming that returns are maximized and costs minimized. Subsidies for all types of economic activity—government sponsored or private—are suspect and are seen as undermining the goal of efficiency. Thus, the study of the "grants economy" by Kenneth Boulding and others is considered offbeat, if not subversive.

Beginning in the sixties, New Left economists began to question whether or not "efficiency," as conventionally defined by the mainstream economists, was either a legitimate goal or an apt description of the typical operation of the advanced capitalist system at *both* macroeconomic and microeconomic levels. The goal of maximizing profits was not necessarily synonymous with greater efficiency, as assumed by neoclassical economic theory.[2] The social cost of this profit-maximizing system was presumably an increasing alienation of labor, a dual labor market, deteriorating living standards for workers, and growing waste.

In my view, the New Left case against mainstream economics is strongest with regard to the United States' inability to solve the macroeconomic problem of providing full employment with minimal inflation. In contrast with its rhetoric, the advanced capitalist system in operation seems to be failing to provide anything resembling full employment. Each year the percentage of the available labor force engaged in productive labor declines, and each year governments tolerate higher levels of unemployed labor and capital. This is true not only in the United States and Canada, but also in other OECD countries. While this double-digit unemployment in OECD countries has brought down the rate of inflation—as posited by the traditional Phillips curve—it represents a tremendous macroeconomic inefficiency.

At the microeconomic level, however, the operation of most United States firms would appear to be remarkably efficient. This is particularly true in comparison with enterprises operating under actually existing socialist conditions, and it is also true in comparison with firms in other advanced capitalist economies. The failure of the United States government to guarantee some sort of safety net, or floor below which citizens cannot be permitted to fall, does indeed serve as a powerful incentive for many individuals to perform in an enterprising manner both within and outside the law. This, in turn, is conducive to the relative efficiency of the firm. On the other hand, the inefficiency in the operation of the noncapitalist enterprise seems somehow to be related to the economic security of workers and to the risk avoidance provided by the routinization of planned investment. This is in contrast with the relative efficiency of these governments in providing full employment with minimal inflation at the macroeconomic level.[3] To be sure, opposition to the goal of efficiency in the capitalist firm has been provided by traditional job-conscious, employment-creating trade unions in the United States, but their influence seems to be waning over time.

In the first two chapters, we will examine the operation of actually existing capitalism at both macroeconomic and microeconomic levels of economic activity. We will pay particular attention to the goal of efficiency and to the role of discrimination at each level.[4] At the macroeconomic level, it is posited that an *increase* in discrimination or segregation is employment-creating and thus absorbs some of the surplus generated by the advanced capitalist system, thereby giving only the illusion of "efficiency" at this level. On the other hand, at the microeconomic level, the *reduction* of discrimination is employment-saving and therefore represents a more "efficient" use of resources at this level. Thus, what we are saying about discrimination can be generally applied to any of the many forms of "disguised" or covert unemployment: there is a trade-off between overt and covert unemployment. During the eighties, Western European countries and Canada have been doing a better job with respect to minimizing covert unemployment, while the United States and Japan have superior records when it comes to minimizing overt unemployment. However, the entire advanced capitalist system tends to display a bias towards employment-creating at the macroeconomic level and employment-saving at the microeconomic level.

STATE&
DISCRIMINATION

The Other Side of the Cold War

1

Scarcity or Surplus:
Which Is the Problem?

While there are numerous contemporary schools of thought in economics, there are essentially two broad paradigms. The more conventional "no free lunch" (NFL) paradigm is held by most mainstream, traditional economists in the United States, from Milton Friedman to Lester Thurow. But it is also held by many Marxists, and is present in the version of Marxism practiced today in the USSR itself.[1] It is sometimes summarized by saying that "there is no such thing as a free lunch" (Friedman) or that we are living in a "zero-sum society" (Thurow). In their view, which can be labeled the "either . . . or" paradigm, increases in one type of economic activity must occur at the expense of some other type of activity. A universal assumption of scarcity and of the need for greater efficiency underlie this mode of thought.

The alternative paradigm can be most clearly found in Bowles, Gordon, and Weisskopf's *Beyond the Wasteland*, which is in the tradition of Baran and Sweezy's *Monopoly Capital*, and might be labeled the "free lunch" (FL) approach.[2] Since there seems to be a growing gap between the *potential* output of our economy and its *actual* performance, a gain in one sector need not be at the expense of another. In fact, we can indeed have our cake and eat it too by putting back to work resources that otherwise would have remained unemployed or underemployed. We might label this the "both . . . and" approach to economic problems. An assumption of relative surplus and of the need for surplus absorption underlie this way of thinking. Under such conditions, the need for greater efficiency is certainly less pressing, if not altogether problematic.

The real roots of the NFL paradigm can be traced back as far as Adam Smith and the classical school, which held that the ultimate goal of a rational economy would either be the provision of more useful goods and services, or additional voluntary leisure. If the goal were the consumption of useful goods and services, then work or employment, especially in the investment sector, was simply a means to accomplish an end. There was no nonsense here about work being a "first necessity of life," as later posited by Marx for his communist stage of development. The long-range goal in an affluent or stationary society, as posited by John Stuart Mill, would therefore be to minimize workers' employment or the disutility of labor and to maximize utilities or satisfaction obtained from final goods or greater voluntary leisure.

In the foreign trade sector, according to the classical school, no particular advantage could be achieved by exporting more than a country imported, as the earlier mercantilist school had advocated. This is because exports were created by the disutility of domestic employment, and imports of useful goods and services were the only possible fruits of international trade for society as a whole. The mercantilists, as well as today's exchange rate mercantilists or "fair traders," have thus put the cart before the horse. They propose the maximization of disutility (work in the export sector) and the minimization of utility, or satisfaction, for society as a whole through the restriction of imports.

In all respects, the NFL approach is employment-saving rather than employment-creating. The act of saving is itself considered to be a virtue since it is assumed that saving is necessary for capital accumulation, and ultimately for higher consumption, to take place. Say's Law is assumed to operate to the extent that no general problem of overproduction (or underconsumption) is conceivable.[3] Government spending or saving is considered to be the only alternative to private spending or saving. In other words, it is inconceivable that there should be any permanent or increased underutilization of resources, or equilibrium at less than full employment, as an alternative. To the extent that government spending and saving (deficits requiring sales of government bonds) impinges upon private spending or saving, there is supposedly a "crowding out" of the latter as a consequence of a capital shortage and rising interest rates.

Greater efficiency is the magical tonic for the NFL system of ideas. Nevertheless, what should be the employment-saving impact of greater efficiency is frequently twisted by NFLers to become on balance employment-creating. For example, according to a *Wall Street Journal* editorial:

> Efficiency creates wealth. Additional wealth broadens the range of things people buy. The new jobs created are more numerous than the jobs lost through improved efficiency. (May 18, 1983)

The key activity responsible for improved efficiency is investment, which supposedly requires prior saving. If investment takes place, productivity increases and the United States becomes more competitive and dominant in world markets. In a NFL economy, consumption is curtailed through the imposition of a sales tax. This constraint on consumption results in increased investment.[4] Only in the distant future may the results of increased efficiency trickle down to ordinary consumers at the bottom.

The origins of the FL paradigm can be traced back to the Great Depression, which ultimately brought forth the Keynesian revolution. Say's Law had indeed broken down, and advanced capitalism seemed to be suffering from the problem of general overproduction, or underconsumption. This was obvious even to non-Marxists. As the private sector deteriorated, the only answer seemed to be an increase in the role of government spending and saving. At first it was thought that the active role of government need only be temporary. But when President Roosevelt cut back on government spending and saving in 1937, the private sector failed to respond positively, and the sharp 1937–38 recession ensued.[5] Only in fascist Germany, Japan, and Italy, where classical Keynesian economics was first boldly applied, did the advanced capitalist system get back to anything resembling full employment before World War II.[6] Full employment was also ostensibly an early characteristic of the noncapitalist system of the USSR. This developed through planned investment which began with the First Five-Year Plan (1927–28 to 1932). However, covert unemployment continued in rural areas for some time thereafter.

Faced with massive unemployment, the new FL approach was necessarily employment-creating rather than employment-saving. Attitudes toward saving also changed drastically. There was a "paradox of thrift," which meant that under certain circumstances saving was, in fact, counterproductive. Because resources were being underutilized, additional saving only made matters worse. By lowering the rate of saving, there would be a larger multiplier effect and a faster return to full employment.[7] And at full employment, a greater *aggregate* amount of saving would be forthcoming. Ironically, the attempt to save more would result in more unemployment and a smaller aggregate amount of saving, and the attempt to save less and spend more—the "paradox of spendthrift"—would result in more employment and a greater aggregate amount of saving.[8]

It was also recognized that saving was rather passive, and that the active variable was investment, which might occur despite what seemed to be limited saving in the eyes of the banking community. In the process of expansion, savings would naturally grow out of higher incomes from formerly underutilized resources. The result would be a "crowding in" of savings as the economy expanded.[9] Under such circumstances, underutilized resources simply represent disguised, or covert, saving.

With the recognition that it was active investment, rather than passive saving, that mattered most, theorists speculated as to why investment was so weak. Either the expected rate of return on capital investment had fallen or the cost of borrowing, as reflected in the interest rate, had failed to fall far enough to accommodate the decline in the expected rate of return. Secular stagnationists such as Alvin Hansen emphasized the decline in population growth (and reduced immigration following the restrictive 1920 legislation), the saturation of domestic markets, the overhang of excess capacity, and perhaps even a slowdown in the rate of technological change. Keynes himself felt that there was a so-called "liquidity trap," meaning that banking authorities and investors' preferences for liquidity tended to hold up real interest rates rather than letting them fall far enough.[10]

Under these circumstances, employment-creating institutions developed which restricted participation rates of the labor force and/or encouraged work sharing. The result was to spread the existing jobs, which were scarce, among more people. Quite naturally, there were more dependents per worker since fewer people had jobs. The newly introduced Social Security System restricted pension payments to older wage earners making less than a certain small amount. This encouraged the "voluntary" early retirement of those between sixty-five and seventy-two years of age, after which restrictions on earned wage income ceased. The Fair Labor Standards Act of 1938 legislated the forty-hour workweek and required that higher rates be paid for overtime work, thereby discouraging the employment of workers for more than the maximum workweek. Great pressure was put on women and blacks to give up their jobs to white male workers. If a female teacher married, she was naturally expected to stop teaching. Thus, certain occupations which formerly had been reserved for women and blacks were integrated, or became exclusively white male occupations.[11] A civil service requirement that there be only one civil servant per family resulted in wives giving up their jobs in about three-fourths of the families affected. In short, this was a decade of disaffirmative, employment-creating action.[12]

During World War II, President Roosevelt was forced briefly to practice classical Keynesian economics, which was already being used by his adversaries with great success. World War II transformed overall United States policy from one of employment-creation to one of employment-saving. The United States entered the war with greatly underutilized resources—both capital and labor—and huge amounts of surplus agricultural products, a result of the stockpiling activities of the Agricultural Adjustment Administration. One of the first steps in accomplishing the wartime Keynesian miracle was the elimination in early 1942 of the power of the Federal Reserve Board to cool off an overheated economy. This was something that the Fed had done as recently as 1936–37 and was a factor which contributed to the 1937–38 recession.[13] Henceforth, money interest rates would be pegged at 2 percent or less. Fiscal policy could now be highly expansive, with minimal tax rate increases to finance surging military expenditures.

As a result, unprecedented federal deficit financing took place. This included both voluntary and virtually compulsory bond sales to the public and monetization of the remaining debt by the newly neutralized Fed. By the end of the war, the national debt stood 25 percent higher than the gross national product of those years, and the monetary base had expanded significantly. Even with the premature lifting of price and wage controls by a Republican-controlled Congress in 1946, there was comparatively little wartime and postwar inflation in the forties, certainly much less than there would be in the stagflating seventies.[14] While the United States ceased the production of civilian automobiles for four years, the per capita consumption of most foods was considerably higher in 1945 than it had been before or since the war. Consequently, total consumption per capita actually rose in the United States during World War II.[15]

Since World War II had been the chief factor ending the

Great Depression, many world economists expected that the postwar period would witness a return to an employment-creating society—one with tendencies toward recession and/or depression. There were two outstanding exceptions to this expectation: the non-Keynesian Arthur Burns in the United States and the Hungarian-born Marxist, Eugene Varga, writing in the USSR. Burns's reputation as an economist was greatly enhanced by subsequent events, but Varga, who believed that the managers of the advanced capitalist system had learned how to stabilize the economy during the war, was ostracized by the Soviet economics establishment until after Stalin's death in 1953.[16]

In contrast to the aftermath of World War I, there was no immediate postwar recession. Price and wage controls had been much more effective during World War II than during World War I. The resulting "pent up" demand and forced saving smoothed the transition to a peacetime economy. In addition, because the Treasury was concerned with servicing the huge national debt as cheaply as possible, the Fed was required to accommodate growth by continually pegging money interest rates throughout the forties and early fifties.[17] Since double-digit inflation occurred between 1946 and 1948, the real interest rate was highly negative in the immediate postwar years. The rate was minimal thereafter, averaging 1 or 2 percent over three decades, until it surged to 6 percent or more during the Reagan era.[18]

The Keynesian revolution throws some light on the intractable reparations problem after World War I. Whereas Keynes's *Economic Consequences of Peace* in 1919 had emphasized the inability of postwar Germany to pay the $30 billion reparations bill called for by the Versailles Treaty, the implications of the *General Theory* in 1936, as recognized by Etienne Mantoux, were very different. One could now place the blame for the earlier reparations fiasco on either the inability of our allies to accept reparations from postwar Germany, or on the inability of the United States to absorb repayment for wartime loans to Great Britain and France.[19]

Although Stalin had been promised $10 billion in reparations from Germany at both the Yalta and Potsdam Conferences, all German reparations were ultimately levied in 1946 on what was then the "Soviet zone," with the blessing of United States Secretary of State, Jimmy Byrnes. Between 1946 and 1953, approximately 20 percent of the East German gross national product was simply siphoned off to the USSR to assist in the rebuilding of the devastated Soviet economy.

Rather than attempting to extract employment-saving reparations from the defeated powers—West Germany and Japan—United States policy makers came up with a scheme more appropriate for the advanced capitalist system when war damage to the economy is minimal. This was the employment-creating Marshall Plan for Western Europe, which included the non-Soviet zones of Germany. Thus, roughly $13 billion worth of useful goods and services made a one-way trip to Western Europe. In effect, the victor was giving reparations to some of the losers in Western Europe. In Asia, once the Japanese economy had recovered and begun to grow again, Japan paid employment-creating reparations to countries it had occupied in World War II, with the exception of China.[20]

At about the same time, President Truman announced a "Point Four" program to assist the Greek monarchy in defeating its native Communists in the post-bellum civil war. The Keynesian employment-creating institution of foreign aid in all of its forms, including Public Law 480, was thus born. It was later adopted by other advanced capitalist countries as a means of disposing of unneeded surpluses (given the domestic unequal distribution of income) and of stimulating domestic employment and profits.[21]

This was only the first in a long series of domestic employment-creating developments. They were either conscious innovations by the state or evolutionary changes in market institutions, and their purpose was either to fetter domestic productivity or to artificially stimulate domestic or foreign consump-

tion of the growing surplus. Table 1 lists some of these developments on the "employment-creating" side of the ledger. At the
same time, there is an "employment-saving" set of institutional
developments. These are generally applicable to the contemporary Soviet-type system, where there truly is no free
lunch.

Note the asterisks on both sides of Table 1. In the left
column, the asterisked items occur in the United States despite
the fact that they are inconsistent with the typical employment-
creating movements taking place after the Keynesian revolution, particularly since World War II. As will be explained in
Chapter 2, both the entry of women into the labor force and
the reduction of discrimination represent more efficient, or
employment-saving, uses of resources. In the right column, the
daggered items are taking place in the USSR despite the fact
that they go against the typical employment-saving movements
which began to characterize the Soviet Union once underutilized resources had been mobilized (i.e., once they had reached
their "intensive" as opposed to the "extensive" stage of development).

On balance, United States capital was exported and labor
(legal and illegal) was imported in order to maintain factor proportions conducive to wage and profit rates which were more
acceptable for the stabilization of the advanced capitalist system. In this manner, the realization problem so evident during
the Great Depression was largely avoided; however, as we shall
see, there later developed a "creeping realization problem" as
secular underutilization grew.

Some of these developments may have actually contributed
to *both* the retardation of the productivity potential and the
certification, or stimulation, of consumption. The development
of the military-industrial complex after the acceptance of the
principles of National Security Council Confidential Document
#68 in 1950 may seem to fit nicely into the category of state in-
novations which stabilized the advanced capitalist system.[22] At
least one study of seventeen industrial nations has argued that

Table 1

A Comparison of NFL and FL Economic Institutional Development

NFL Employment-saving, or "rational," developments	*FL Employment-creating, or "irrational," developments*
1. Increased productivity (automation or robotization).	1. Decreased productivity (featherbedding).
2. Receiving of reparations or foreign aid, or parsimonious giver of aid.	2. Giving of foreign aid or reparations after war (Export-Import Bank and DISC subsidies).
3. Emphasis on importation of goods and services and on receiving of foreign investment or loans.	3. Emphasis on exportation of goods and services or making foreign investment and subsidizing domestic investment via investment tax credit.
4. Increased female labor force participation rates. (Reduced covert unemployment in home.)*	4. Decreased female labor force participation rates. (More covert unemployment in home.)
5. Emphasis on disarmament.	5. Increased military-industrial complex expenditures.†
6. Desegregation and affirmative action.*	6. Segregation and discrimination.
7. Law abidance and capital punishment (use of prison labor to produce useful products).	7. Crime and life imprisonment.
8. Volunteer armed forces.*	8. Draft, or compulsory national service.†
9. Negative income tax and avoidance of welfare establishment; workfare.*	9. Welfare establishment, including food stamps. Special Maternity Allowances.

10. Lack of environmental movement, weak controls over pollution.
11. No installment credit or credit cards.
12. No "Wall Street" operation.
13. Austere product differentiation and minimal advertising.
14. Preventive medicine.
15. Voluntary schooling and retirement.
16. Commercialization of animal husbandry and expansion into "Virgin Lands."
17. Moonlighting encouraged.
18. Strong family ties and extended family living.
19. Stiff prosecution of counterfeiting.
20. Sales, turnover, or value-added tax.
21. Surplus in budget.
22. Decriminalized drugs.

10. Environmental movement.†
11. Installment credit and credit cards.
12. Wall Street and financial sector.
13. Extensive product differentiation, coupons, and redundant advertising.
14. Overmedication, including unnecessary surgery.
15. Compulsory schooling and early retirement.
16. Animal liberation movement and soil banks.
17. Work sharing arrangements.
18. Divorce and separate living conditions.†
19. Relaxed attitude toward counterfeiting or "do-it-yourself" monetary policy.
20. Personal income tax, with "long form" as employment creator for accountants, and "do-it-yourself" fiscal policy.
21. Deficits in budget.
22. Illegal drugs and attempts to restrict supplies.

* Indicates antithetical to stabilization in the United States.
† Indicates antithetical to growth in the USSR.

military spending is associated with a lower share of investment and reduced growth.[23]

In the United States, however, increased defense expenditures and greater investment occurred almost simultaneously during the Kennedy administration. This was a result of the relatively slack economy inherited from President Eisenhower and his pre-Keynesian policies. In fact, the rise in defense spending may have occurred slightly prior to the increase in investment, since it was not until 1962 that accelerated depreciation was institutionalized and the investment tax credit was introduced as a thinly disguised subsidy for investment. Significant increases in defense spending occurred shortly after the confrontation between Kennedy and Khrushchev at Vienna during the first half of 1961. As a result of the investment tax credit and the institutionalization of accelerated depreciation practices, Walter Heller, then Kennedy's Chairman of the Council of Economic Advisers, could later legitimately label himself as the first practicing supply-side economic policy maker of the postwar era.[24]

The attitude of trade unions toward automation has continued to be negative since World War II.[25] As jobs become harder to find, the propensity toward featherbedding by unions has become greater over time. Trade unions have not had too much success in reducing the average workweek in manufacturing since World War II, although labor spokespersons have made frequent proposals for an official thirty-five hour workweek without reductions in weekly pay.[26] Robotization of routine assembly line jobs has required that union collective bargainers pay more attention to job security than to increases in wages.

Even leisure—both voluntary and involuntary—has taken on an employment-creating bias. Instead of pursuing better interpersonal relations, listening to or making music, writing poetry, and participating in athletics for sheer enjoyment, we have substituted frantic domestic and international travel and the commercialization of highly competitive spectator sports, including sexual relations. The unemployed, who are suffering from involuntary leisure, are poorly covered by unemployment compensation, and this has resulted in a mushrooming of make-work activities in the second, or underground, economy.[27]

The ideology behind Reaganomics and the ardent supply-side economics of the Polyconomics people can be seen as an attempt to revert to a pre-Keynesian NFL paradigm. According to the supply-siders, there is no problem today with the operation of Say's Law; saving can be safely encouraged since it is once again a necessary precondition for investment. There is a relaxed attitude toward the large and growing import surplus. This includes attempts to reduce the budget of the Export-Import Bank, elimination of DISCs, and a general questioning of foreign aid.[28]

To the credit of some supply-siders sympathetic to the Reagan administration, such as Representative Jack Kemp, there has also been some recognition of the possible role of the Fed in creating the stagnation and creeping realization problem which began in 1966. But the proposed solution to this problem is the same as that of the nineteenth century, when employment-saving supply-side economics prevailed worldwide: the restoration of the international gold standard.[29]

The problem with this attempt to turn the clock back to the nineteenth century is that it overlooks the comparatively intimate relationship between investment and consumption in the advanced capitalist system. The implication of our earlier flirtation with supply-side economics in the Kennedy-Johnson years was that a policy of stimulating investment without significant regard for consumption seemed only to produce good macro-economic results in the short run and excess capacity in the long run.

From 1962 to 1966, accelerated depreciation and the investment tax credit resulted in an investment binge and almost full employment. The Johnson tax cut in 1964—like its Kemp-Roth imitation in the Reagan era—was nonprogressive in that it largely benefited those in the upper income groups, the potential savers.[30] To the amazement of some, it also produced a very nearly balanced budget in 1965 as government revenue poured in from previously underutilized labor and capital. At one point in 1966, the "new economists" of the Council of Economic Advisers were optimistically predicting that the future problem of the federal government would be to find new ways in which to spend the projected revenue bonanza expected from potential budget surpluses.

As mentioned above, 1966 was the peak year of euphoria over the "new economics," or what we now more fashionably call supply-side economics. Subsequently, disproportionality and underutilization of resources again reared their ugly heads. The Vietnam War was the first war fought at less than full employment and, in fact, with two recessions. Capacity utilization rates began to fall after 1966, and lower profit rates during the war also reflected our failure to utilize productive capacity efficiently.

The Federal Reserve Board only added to the difficulties of the fiscal policy makers. This was particularly obvious in December 1965, when the Fed stepped sharply on the monetary brakes before the Council of Economic Advisers could bring forth their recommendations for the application of fiscal brakes in the form of tax rate increases. A confrontation between the chairman of the Fed, William McChesney Martin, and the Council of Economic Advisers, which took place on the Pedernales in Texas, produced something of a stalemate with but two minor tax increases: the brief elimination of the investment tax credit and the application of progressive rather than proportional, or flat, tax rates to the current withholding tax. Still, there ensued both a monetary crunch of significant proportions and a growth recession, or minirecession, covering the last two quarters of 1966 and the first two quarters of 1967.[31] Since the increase in Vietnam military spending during this period was greater than planned, some Wall Street economists concluded erroneously that wartime military spending had lost its magic touch in producing prosperity.[32]

As a general rule, the Fed prides itself on the fact that its monetary policies "lean against the wind." If fiscal policy is easy, then the Fed feels justified in tightening the screws on the money supply. The problem is that the Fed almost always views fiscal policy as being expansionary and therefore alternates between "tight" and "very tight" monetary policy. Interest rates rise quite easily, but are very sticky on the downside. As a result, the Fed has in effect imposed its own "incomes policy" on the rest of the economy. Net interest as a share of total income has risen from less than 1 percent in the late forties to over 8 percent in the early eighties. The real interest rate has risen from minus 7 percent to plus 7 percent in the past forty years.[33]

The justification for Fed policies is the assumption that there is too much money and credit in the system and, that by restricting the money supply, inflationary pressures can be reduced. In fact, however, since the Treasury Accord of March 1951 and the resurrection of active Federal Reserve monetary policy, the real money supply (as measured by deflated M-1) has grown more slowly than the real gross national product, thus requiring a secular 3 percent per annum increase in the velocity of money, or the rapidity of its turnover, until 1981.[34] If we were suffering from demand-pull inflation, there might be some justification for the Fed's policy, but high real interest rates in a period of supply-side inflation simply push up costs and prices even further. Treating a sick patient with the wrong prescription has hardly improved the overall health of the economy.

Despite the negative, employment-creating picture of the United States economy since World War II, there are at least two shining examples of movement toward greater efficiency and employment-saving which are at variance with the other systemic developments (items 4 and 6 of the NFL model in Table 1). These are the increased labor force participation rates for United States women and the affirmative action programs for all minorities including women, who have all of the economic characteristics of minorities.[35] In the next chapter, we shall examine these atypical employment-saving developments and hypothesize as to the reasons for these changes which seem to be at cross-purposes with the FL economy and its non-progressive employment-creating laws of motion.

2

The Microeconomics of Discrimination

Discrimination in production, or on the supply side of the market, may be narrowly defined as the hiring of labor on the basis of some characteristic other than productivity.[1] In the past, and to a great extent today, this has meant that white males have frequently been hired in preference to persons of color or females despite the fact that *at the margin* the non-whites or females not hired were potentially more productive and/or more highly motivated. As a result of this discrimination, actual productivity was lower than potential productivity, and actual costs were higher than potentially lower costs. It can also be assumed that the discriminatory employer would not survive in any competitive market if competing enterprises were non-discriminatory in the hiring and promotion of workers.

Thus, we can see the theoretical basis for the observable fact that the white capitalist has ultimately welcomed government affirmative action programs since they require him or her to hire more productive workers and to operate more efficiently with higher profits.[2] The employer's "taste for profits" overwhelms any possible "taste for discrimination." By the same token, we should not be too surprised to find that labor unions, which are frequently white male-dominated institutions that protect the weaker, or marginal, members of the group (those with lower productivity), have typically dragged their collective feet with respect to such programs.[3] The black capitalist, like the white male trade unionist, is also hurt to some extent by the breakdown of discrimination and segregation since his/her enterprise, which caters largely to a protected market, has been making profits by operating in this relatively noncompetitive environment.[4]

The upshot of this position, which was first developed in 1957 by Gary Becker of the Chicago NFL school, is that discrimination and discriminatory practices are employment-creating. The breakdown of such practices will be employment-saving and therefore more efficient for the firm, as well as for society as a whole, *if* the resources saved can be utilized at the macroeconomic level.[5] In other words, it has taken more white males to produce the same product which might have been produced by a combination of fewer people that included nonwhites or females.

The inefficiency associated with discrimination is frequently used as a basis for calculating what gross national product might be if there were no discriminatory practices. Naturally, this exercise produces a *calculated* higher GNP without discrimination, but it is virtually pointless unless some attention is also paid to the distribution problem.[6] The underlying problem of the advanced capitalist system is not so much one of becoming more efficient, as the NFLers would have us believe, as it is one of distributing all that we are capable of producing. The Chicago NFL school argues that employers are indulging in an ahistorical "taste for discrimination," which is only made possible by a noncompetitive market or monopoly positions. Its prescription for eliminating discrimination is to break down the oligopolistic market structures in the United States and to create or restore the competitive market of the neoclassical model. The Chicago school's attitude toward the government's antitrust activity is thus not too different from the position of Gabriel Kolko. In the name of preserving or restoring competition, the state has, in effect, been doing the opposite: protecting larger production units from domestic "cutthroat" competition and from dumping from abroad.

In their praise of free competitive markets as a force that could eliminate discrimination, Sowell et al. make no distinction between types of markets, although they do recognize that the greatest progress for minorities has taken place during wartime, when sellers' markets for labor have prevailed. In their view, there is no increasing tendency for the operation of the free market to produce buyers' markets in which purchasers of labor power are able to pick and choose among many available candidates for the job. The ideal free market referred to by Sowell and his colleagues was most closely approximated in the decade of the twenties, when government and trade union intervention were at a low in the United States. This situation eventually brought forth the macroeconomic problem of the Great Depression and the extreme buyers' market of the thirties.

For this reason, it was important for Milton Friedman and the Chicago school to come up with some *bête noire* other than the relatively free market conditions of the twenties in order to explain the depth of the Great Depression. In pointing to poor monetary policy decisions by the Fed in the early thirties or Smoot-Hawley protectionism after 1930, Friedman certainly has a point in the exacerbation of the problem. But why did the same economic catastrophe take place throughout the advanced capitalist system?

In the last analysis, the crisis was most severe in precisely the one country where Friedmanian neoclassical prescriptions were applied most vigorously—Germany. When the Bruening government convinced German workers to take a 10 percent pay cut, Germany ended up with over 30 percent unemployment rather than the 25 percent that Roosevelt's New Deal inherited from Herbert Hoover.[7] In substance, it was the use of the neoclassical solution of cutting wages to reduce unemployment that created the conditions favorable for the election of Adolph Hitler. This occurred in the same year that the New Deal launched what eventually became a successful effort to rescue the advanced capitalist system from its realization crisis.

The practice of providing segregated facilities, as in South

African apartheid (or as formerly practiced by the United States armed forces until 1948, and in "separate but equal" schools in southern states until after 1954), is likewise wasteful of resources, despite the fact that it is undoubtedly employment-creating in a FL environment. The providing of separate restaurants, washrooms, educational facilities, and sleeping quarters is clearly a wasteful expenditure of capital. Neither white nor black facilities are likely to be used to their maximum capabilities. Therefore, extra, or redundant, capital—including additional capital for transportation—must be provided to service the segregated labor forces.[8]

It is not surprising to find that white capitalists—whether they represent northern capital moving from the northeast to the south after World War II or the white multinational corporation expanding its operations in South Africa in the postwar years—view separate facilities as inefficient institutions that waste capital and reduce potential profits. Conversely, white trade unionists in these two areas would undoubtedly resist the elimination of segregation.[9]

The rapid entry of women and blacks into the industrial labor force during the overfull employment conditions of World War II seemed only natural, for it simply reproduced what had already occurred during World War I. Whenever there were more than enough jobs for all, women and blacks were not as strongly objected to in the job market and were even provided with government-operated child care facilities. After the war, when the spectre of another Great Depression arose, government child care facilities were dissolved, and women were expected to return to the home, where they contributed their talents and energies to the postwar baby boom.[10]

What is unexpected and needs explaining is the steady increase in female labor force participation rates in the United States, particularly after 1966, when unemployment and slack began to grow in a secular, or long-term, fashion.[11] Coincidentally, the baby bust, which produced fertility rates below those needed to maintain the domestic population in the long run, also began at about this time. One might conclude that both of these occurrences are somehow related to the improvement in contraceptive technology, particularly the introduction of oral contraceptives. However, in at least four advanced capitalist countries—the Federal Republic of Germany, Switzerland, Austria, and Japan—female labor force participation rates have been reduced in recent years as growing unemployment problems have once again put pressure on women to relinquish their jobs to men.[12] In such cases, the reentry of women into domestic production represents an institutional development whose employment-creating effects favor male workers.

It may not be obvious why the entry of women into commodity production represents a movement toward greater efficiency, or employment-saving, for the economy as a whole. The job of being a housewife and caring for children represents a great deal of covert unemployment that becomes reduced, or even eliminated, when women work away from the home.[13] On the demand side, there appears to be an increasing technological bias toward the creation of jobs that do not require brawn, thus female labor becomes more desirable from the standpoint of the employer. The fact that female labor is frequently subject to discrimination, and is therefore often less militant, only adds an important fillip to the employer's demand for ex-housewives.

While discrimination against blacks and women decreased significantly as a result of the overfull employment conditions of World War II, the war itself was largely fought with segregated armies and navies, and endemic racism. The war was also fought with the majority of our Japanese-Americans in concentration camps, and it was ended by dropping atomic bombs on Japanese cities. Thus, it wasn't until July 1948 that President Truman gave the memorable order which eventually forced the recalcitrant armed forces to think seriously about desegregating their operations.

Since then, the armed services—a growth sector subject to a sellers' market for labor—have been in the vanguard when it comes to opening up opportunities for minorities, including, eventually, women.[14] President Truman's decision represents a break between the time when the federal government tended to pursue a frequently racist policy and when it became a leading agent in breaking down racial segregation and discrimination. To understand the basis for the Truman decision to reverse state policy with respect to segregation, it is necessary to examine the political climate of those times. In 1948, President Truman was being attacked from both sides of the Democratic coalition forged by President Roosevelt. The attack from his right came from the Dixiecrats led by Strom Thurmond, and the pressure from the left came from the Progressive Party led by Henry Wallace. Wallace had been Roosevelt's vice-president from 1941 to 1945, as well as a cabinet member both before and after the war. The Cold War with the Soviet Union was just beginning, and the issue of relations with the USSR represented one of the points dividing the Truman centrists from the Wallace Progressives. Thus, both the decision to integrate the armed forces and the liberal platform of the newly spawned Americans for Democratic Action were clearly designed to attract liberal and black Democrats back into the regular party. Truman's centrists favored a tougher policy with respect to the USSR as opposed to Wallace and his Progressives, who resisted universal military training and urged the continuation of the wartime detente with the Soviet Union.[15] This liberalization of domestic policy, accompanied by a bellicose foreign policy, was also evident in the Nixon years, when the welfare state expanded rapidly while the administration pursued an unpopular foreign policy.

The debates among the presidential candidates throw some light on the pressures for change at the time. At one point, Norman Thomas, the perennial candidate of the anti-Communist Socialist party, asked Wallace how he distinguished "except in racism, between the tactics of fascism and communist totalitarianism." Wallace replied: "that 'except for racism' tells a great deal of the story." In February 1948, the Secretary of the Army, Kenneth Royall, argued that the regular army would

continue to segregate "in the interest of national defense."
Later, General Eisenhower supported army segregation in a
statement before the Senate Armed Services Committee on
April 2, 1948.[16] But, by July 26, 1948, in response to Wallace's
charges that Truman was a "segregationist," Truman set up the
Presidential Committee on Equality of Treatment and Opportunity in the Armed Forces, headed by Charles Fahy. In a
September 12, 1948 broadcast over NBC, Wallace observed
that racial prejudice and segregation "can cost America its
life. . . . The eyes of the world are upon us, assessing our treatment of Negroes and other minorities, and they ask: what do
Southern Americans really mean by democracy?"[17] Because of
the ambiguity of Truman's charges to the committee, Wallace
was still urging the president "to take pen in hand and sign an
order abolishing segregation in the armed forces" in October,
just before the election.

The decision to integrate United States society in general
was very useful, for it supported the United States' continued
and growing influence upon Third World countries which were
mostly nonwhite and were beginning to liberate themselves
from the directly colonial type of Western imperialism. Subsequently, competition with the Russians for influence among
the world's nonwhites has served as the underlying basis for the
continuity and lack of volatility in the racial and sexual posture
of the United States government since 1948.

The link between improved race relations and United States
policy was recognized by a number of important people during
the course of World War II. The most influential social scientist
to note this was the Swedish Nobel Prize winner, Gunnar Myrdal, in his monumental opus, *An American Dilemma*. According
to David W. Southern, who has made an exhaustive study of the
impact of Myrdal's research:

> Many international-minded Americans realized that their na-
> tion's rise to world leadership necessitated changes in race re-
> lations at home. The cosmopolitan Myrdal displayed an espe-

cially keen insight into the foreign relations aspect of the race problem. In the final chapter of the *Dilemma*, he warned America that her world prestige and future security would hinge on how the race problem was handled. Deeply suspicious of the Soviet Union, the Swedish scholar foresaw the coming of the Cold War as soon as World War II began. Owing to the international rising tide of colored peoples, the Soviets, Myrdal predicted, would woo the non-white nations of the world with a flood of egalitarian propaganda. If the United States hoped to make the "American Century" a reality, Myrdal maintained, she would have to persuade the world that she truly believed in equality, regardless of color.[18]

Others who recognized the relationship between race and our postwar international relations included Henry Luce, publisher of *Time* magazine, and presidential candidate Wendell Willkie. According to Willkie in 1944, "Every time some race-baiter ill-treats some man in America, he lessens the ability of America to lead the world to freedom." During the war, W. E. B. DuBois recognized this upcoming struggle and was later to press the point before the United Nations. As a newspaper columnist during the war, he wrote:

> Equally there is no doubt that Willkie and Wallace see the color line as the first line of offense in the world struggle. When we have conquered Hitler, then the real battle for the Allies will begin, in the effort to conquer themselves of the habit of despising and exploiting colored folk.[19]

Shortly after the war, E. H. Carr recognized the role of the Soviets in influencing Western democracies. In his Oxford University lectures he stated:

> The equality preached in the Soviet Union is not an equality of function or an equality of reward. . . . But, equality, in the sense in which it is one of the fundamental purposes of Soviet social policy, means nondiscrimination between human beings on irrelevant grounds such as sex, race, color, or class. Soviet

principles and practices compare favorably in this respect with
those of some democratic countries. One effect of the Soviet
impact on these countries has been an increased recognition of
the irrelevance of such barriers and a strengthened demand to
sweep them away.[20]

Most recently, the American Council on Education has once
again recognized the Soviet challenge:

> Today, a growing majority of the world's people themselves
> are Asian, Latin, and black. They are subject to competing
> claims about which system best produces material plenty, so-
> cial justice, and freedom—that of the Western democracies, or
> that of the Eastern socialist bloc. We Americans know and
> argue, that our model holds the greatest promise for these
> emerging peoples; that we march under the banner of true so-
> cial justice. However, the credibility of our claim depends in
> large part on our ability to demonstrate that our system pro-
> vides full equality and full participation to all our citizens, in-
> cluding those of color.[21]

The Soviet Union has been practicing affirmative action with
respect to its own minorities, including women, since 1917. The
Soviets have attempted to integrate nonwhite Central Asia into
the mainstream of Soviet society. The liberation of women
through such measures as liberal abortion laws beginning in
1920—albeit with a twenty-year hiatus between 1936 and
1956—may have influenced United States policy makers, including the United States Supreme Court. President Reagan
may go through the motions of attempting to limit "choice" or
even affirmative action, but the exogenous forces affecting the
system—particularly the competition between the superpowers—guarantees that as long as the Cold War continues, it
will be difficult to turn the clock back to the situation that existed before World War II.[22] In this connection, it must be
assumed that the Soviets remain true to their ideology, which
stresses egalitarianism, and that the United States continues to

reject isolationism and a Fortress U.S.A. mentality.

It is sometimes mistakenly assumed that the New Deal had a benevolent influence with respect to minorities.[23] In fact, however, when minimum wages were established under the NIRA in the thirties, there were separate, lower minimums for black and women workers. As a result of the Great Depression, there were fewer blacks employed in manufacturing at the end of the thirties than there were at the beginning of that decade. By the same token, the percentage of professional women dropped from 14.2 to 12.3 percent of all professionals during the thirties.[24] Many occupations formerly dominated by blacks and females were taken back by white males because of the serious overall job shortage. Myrdal pointed out, "as jobs became cleaner, safer, and better paying, whites usually replaced black workers . . . the Agricultural Adjustment Act reduced cotton acreage and pushed black tenants off the land. The National Recovery Act threw many blacks out of work. The Works Progress Administration paid blacks lower wages than whites, and the Federal Housing Administration perpetuated segregated neighborhoods by upholding restrictive covenants."[25]

Eleanor Roosevelt was undoubtedly sincerely sympathetic to the plight of the black population, but President Roosevelt—who primarily chose white southerners, such as Jonathan Daniel, for racial advisers—was forced to pay practical attention to his solid support in the Old South, where racism was endemic. Interior Secretary Harold Ickes and Labor Secretary Frances Perkins were both strongly antiracist in the cabinet, but even Agricultural Secretary Henry Wallace encouraged his black friends to be patient, and he appointed no blacks to positions above the level of clerk in his AAA.[26] If there is any truth to the notion that opposing forces frequently tend to take on each other's characteristics (both positive and negative), one could argue that since the principal enemy before and during the war was Hitler's super-racist Germany (rather than the nonracist USSR), racism was more tolerable domestically.

There were many incipient signs of deterioration in the conditions of blacks before the Great Depression. The secular decline in the black population, from 20 percent of the total United States population at the end of the eighteenth century to 9 percent by the end of the 1920s, reflected the "radical" treatment of blacks in the South, to use a term employed by Joel Williamson.[27] The custom of light blacks passing as whites and the higher incidence of venereal disease among blacks, producing widespread infertility, no doubt helped explain why "radicalism" in the South assumed that "blacks were a doomed and dying race."[28]

The United States economy seemed to be developing without serious realization problems until 1929. The steady flow of immigration into the United States was evidence of this, but it was thwarted finally by restrictive immigration laws in the early twenties. Nevertheless, there were occasional symptoms of overcapacity, overproduction and/or underconsumption, and signs pointing to the usefulness of employment-creating institutions much earlier. It is true that the immediate impact of the Civil War had been integrationist, and it was followed by a twenty-five-year period of relatively benign treatment of blacks. In the North, there was an unprecedented period of racial amity and integration, especially between 1870 and 1890.[29] Beginning around 1890, however, things changed dramatically, particularly in the South. The feeling of paternalism for blacks was replaced by repressive treatment and the growth of segregation. "Jim Crow" conditions became part of employment-creating institutions. The collapsing Southern cotton economy of the late 1880s and early 1890s may have played a role in initiating this turn of events.

Just as suddenly, things improved for blacks in 1915. The prosperity and NFL environment generated by World War I caused blacks to benefit from full employment conditions provided by the loans to Great Britain and France and by the labor shortage created by the growth of the United States armed forces. Blacks themselves were used in the armed forces of World War I on a segregated basis, as was the case in earlier wars. Although black riots and the Galveston massacre were associated with the steep postwar recession, relatively full employment during the decade of the 1920s—a period when the "Harlem Renaissance" blossomed—allowed again for comparatively benign treatment of blacks. The 1920s was also a decade in which black film companies prospered.[30]

In Chapter 3, we shall look more carefully at the ebb and flow of conditions for blacks before 1948 and the volatility of state policy. In Chapter 4, we will examine the comparative lack of volatility and rather steady progress in the slow breakdown of segregation and discrimination after 1948. In so doing, we will attempt to judge the net effect of two forces working in opposite directions. There is an endogenous force (growing underutilization of our productive potential in a FL atmosphere) which might be expected to produce a worsening of conditions for blacks and women and a need for employment-creating institutions such as discrimination and segregation. At the same time, there is an exogenous force (competition with the Russians for the allegiance of the nonwhite Third World) that operates politically in the opposite direction. In examining these forces, we are testing Lenin's dictum that politics overrides economic considerations.

Chapter 5 will look at discrimination and segregation in other advanced capitalist countries—particularly Canada—in comparison with the United States, while Chapter 6 will consider the other side of the coin: the effects of the Soviet competition with the United States on developments within the USSR. Chapter 7 examines the smaller socialist countries of Eastern Europe in general, but with particular emphasis on Hungary and the status of women and Gypsies there. If it is true that the Cold War primarily affects the policies of the United States and the USSR, we would expect to find the minor countries in the two systems—particularly Canada and Hungary—to be more sluggish in their movements toward affirmative action.

3

The Volatility of State Policy Before 1948

Thomas Sowell and other NFLers emphasize the historic volatility, or unreliability, of United States state policy with respect to race. In their view, reliance on the freely competitive market, rather than on the state, is more likely to guarantee that the relative welfare of blacks will improve over time. There has been a great deal of evidence to support state volatility, especially in the nineteenth century. This is particularly true with respect to our ambivalent attitude toward the role of blacks in the armed services until after 1948.

Blacks have been casualties in all of our wars beginning with the death of an escaped slave, Crispus Attucks, the first person to fall in the American Revolution. An estimated five thousand blacks, including those in the Continental Navy and state navies, as well as privateers, fought in the colonial forces of the American Revolution.[1] General Washington's original policy was to exclude blacks from the army, but blacks, most of whom were indentured servants, volunteered and eventually fought on both sides in the revolution. A significant number of blacks fought on the British side since the Crown had promised them their freedom should the revolution be put down. With the defeat of the British, some of these Loyalist blacks settled in Canada.

In the War of 1812, Commodore Perry, like General Washington, originally wanted to exclude blacks from the navy, but changed his mind when he saw the quality performance of black soldiers. In the end, about 25 percent of Commodore Perry's navy was black. Blacks were also heavily represented on the whaling ships of that time.

At the beginning of the Civil War, blacks were denied entry when they attempted to join the Union Army since President Lincoln feared the loss of border states if blacks were allowed to serve. At the beginning of 1863, after the Emancipation Proclamation was issued, the army was officially opened to blacks. However, they were strictly segregated into "National Colored Troops." Toward the end of the war, even the Confederacy was desperate enough to use black troops in labor batallions and in supply services. In all, some thirty-eight thousand blacks made the supreme sacrifice, a mortality rate almost 40 percent higher than that of the white troops.[2] After the war, in the "taming" of the West by the United States Cavalry, many blacks were used in the attempt to subdue Native Americans. In fact, some of General Custer's troops were black.

Blacks played a vital role in the Spanish-American War of 1898. At the outset, twenty blacks lost their lives as a result of the sinking of the Battleship *Maine* on February 15, 1898. Teddy Roosevelt praised the quality of his "colored troops," although years later in peacetime he would condemn several black units for striking against the segregationist attitudes of the army.

During World War I, United States military forces remained segregated, although there were about four hundred thousand black troops in France commanded by white French officers. Despite the discrimination that followed blacks into the trenches, they fought well, particularly the 369th Infantry Regiment, receiving many honors, including the French Coeur de Guerre.

During the interwar years, blacks were reduced to 3 percent of all servicemen, with most blacks segregated into labor batallions. This rigid segregation tended to mirror what was going on in civilian life. By 1940, only five thousand enlisted men and five black officers (three of whom were chaplains) were serving in the armed forces. Benjamin Davis became the first black West Point graduate in 1936, and the Air Force later began training black flyers at Tuskegee Institute in Alabama. It would be early 1941 before these trained pilots were accepted for flight duty in segregated units such as the 99th Fighter Squadron.[3] Ninety-five black pilots were later to win Distinguished Flying Crosses in World War II.

More than one million blacks served in the military in World War II, all over Europe and throughout the Pacific. In the navy, blacks were largely confined to menial jobs such as mess servants. The first regular black navy officer was not commissioned until after World War II. Even black army officers ate separately from whites on trains in the United States. Two all-black infantry units served overseas, one of which (the 92nd "Buffalo" Division in Italy) was accused of cowardice in the face of German troops. Despite these charges, five hundred black men in this unit received the bronze star. After the war, black men and women came home to fight a new struggle—this time for their civil rights.

Our first recognition of the necessity for affirmative action with respect to blacks occurred as a result of the Civil War.[4] The United States Constitution, which originally counted the black male as being equivalent to three-fifths of a man, was amended three times. The Thirteenth Amendment (1865) abolished slavery; the Fourteenth Amendment (1868) established the citizenship of blacks and the requirement of equal protection under our laws; and the Fifteenth Amendment (1870) prohibited abridgement of the right to vote "on account of race, color, or previous condition of servitude."

In addition, the Federal Civil Rights Act of 1866 guaranteed the rights of ex-slaves to make and enforce contracts; the right to buy, sell, and own real and personal property; the right to sue, to be a party in legal actions, and to give evidence; and the right to full and equal benefit of all laws and proceedings for the security of person and estate.

In March, 1865, during the closing months of the Civil War, Congress created the Bureau of Refugees, Freedmen, and Abandoned Lands—the "Freedmen's Bureau"—which provided for employment, education, and housing assistance to newly freed men. Federal support for Howard University (founded in 1867) is a good example of the recognition on the part of the state that special, positive actions were needed to help ex-slaves make the transition to being free men and women. A total of fifteen colleges, including Fisk University, were established under the Bureau. During the Reconstruction years, newly enfranchised black voters elected hundreds of black officials to state and local office and sent two United States Senators and twenty representatives to Congress after 1870.

However, the affirmative action of the Reconstruction Era was relatively short-lived. In 1872, Congress granted a general amnesty restoring full political rights to all but a few white ex-Confederates. The 1876 election of Representative Rutherford B. Hayes to the presidency set the stage for the complete abdication of special federal protection for blacks, including the withdrawal of all federal troops from the South. By 1889, Henry W. Grady, part owner of the *Atlanta Constitution*, would remark that the "Negro as a political force has dropped out of serious consideration." In the 1896 case of *Plessy v. Ferguson*, the United States Supreme Court officially sanctioned government separation and segregation of the races. By the turn of the century, the federal government had abandoned its earlier role as protector of racial minorities. Later, President Woodrow Wilson, the first Southerner to be elected president since the Civil War, even attempted to segregate blacks in the civil service.

While the federal government was pushing affirmative action after the Civil War, the first large-scale exclusion of blacks was perpetrated by a private organization, the National Labor Union, in 1869. Since then, United States unionism has tended to be more "job conscious" than "class conscious," as compared with Western European unionism. In such organizations, which are typically organized along craft lines, the union is concerned only with the allocation of scarce jobs among members, to the exclusion of all others. What is somewhat puzzling about the early "job conscious" union is that it was organized in a period of relative postwar prosperity.[5] Still, it is now clear that between 1870 and 1920 the possibility of unemployment was a fact of everyday existence.[6]

The Knights of Labor, which enjoyed a short existence that ended in 1886, attempted to organize workers of all colors along industrial lines. Its successor, the more successful American Federation of Labor (AF of L), was chiefly interested in skilled workers and, if not actually racist and sexist, was oblivious to racial and sexual problems.[7] As early as 1896, nine years after its inception, the AF of L compromised on the issue of racial equality by admitting deliberately discriminatory unions. By 1899, the AF of L was even admitting unions whose constitution explicitly forbade black membership.[8] Its long-time head, Samuel Gompers, was more interested in expanding the overall power of the trade union and was willing to abandon blacks to do so. The problem with the approach of excluding blacks from United States trade unions was that nonunion blacks were frequently used by employers as strikebreakers. Quite naturally, this reinforced latent racism among white unionists, particularly white ethnic groups recently arrived from Europe.

The International Workers of the World (IWW), which was organized by syndicalists in 1905 and was effectively eliminated by government repression shortly after World War I, took a positive position toward blacks. Likewise, the Congress of Industrial Organization (CIO) began organizing all skilled and unskilled workers in industry, beginning in 1935. However, each was more the exception than the rule in the United States union movement. In many cases, United States Communists played an active role in fighting racism within progressive unions such as those of longshoremen, automobile workers, steel workers, furriers, meat packers, hospital workers, and electrical workers.[9]

Unions have typically been opposed to liberalized immigration laws, particularly if the immigrants are nonwhites. The Chinese, after helping us build our railroads, were considered to be people of sin and immorality and were characterized as having inferior social standards.[10] This seems particularly surprising today since Chinese-Americans are noted chiefly for having lower-than-average crime rates. A union which welcomed immigrants to its ranks in the 1970s was Cesar Chavez's United Farm Workers. This union, however, has subsequently declined in power and importance.

Even United States left-of-center and socialist political parties have either had considerable racism in their histories or have simply neglected the black population. The Populist movement was generally anti-black. Both the Eugene V. Debs Socialists and the Socialist Labor party failed to worry about blacks and their problems.[11] The attempt of the United States Communist Party in the twenties and thirties to organize blacks and develop a program to attract them was thus unique until the establishment of Henry Wallace's Progressive party in 1947.[12] At one point, the United States Communist party developed a program for a separate black state in the "black belt," which was modeled after the Soviet nationality policy for different ethnic groups. The fact that many Communist party members worked within the Progressive party in 1948 only insured that its program would be one of affirmative action toward blacks. Wallace and his running mate, Senator Glen Taylor, refused to speak before segregated audiences in the South in 1948—a pioneer departure from previous political practices.

There is considerable evidence that a good deal of our political volatility with respect to race—at both state and private sector levels—has been related to overall economic conditions, specifically the nature of the labor market. As has already been noted, periods of genuine full employment—ordinarily found only in wartime—have been times when both blacks and women have made considerable headway in achieving greater equality and upward mobility.

On the other hand, periods of recession or depression have been especially difficult years for blacks and women. As mentioned above, the collapse of the cotton economy in the latter part of the nineteenth century coincided with a sudden increase in repression and segregation of blacks, particularly, but not exclusively, in the South. Likewise, the Great Depression was another especially difficult time for blacks.

Some token efforts were made to assist blacks under the New Deal in the thirties. By the implied authority of the National Industrial Recovery Act of 1933, the administrators of the NIRA issued regulations designed to end discrimination in employment and provided for sanctions against violators. However, the industrial codes of this brief period permitted separate lower minimum wages for black workers in the South, and one out of every four industrial codes permitted women to be paid a lower minimum wage than men.[13] The Civilian Conservation Corps was racially integrated at first (although restricted to males), but soon administrators reorganized the CCC according to race, and the representation of blacks in the corps was never proportional to their share of the population.[14] As late as 1938, women did not have the right to a minimum wage in twenty-one out of forty-eight states.

An important agency to encourage segregation was the Federal Housing Authority, established under the New Deal in 1938. For the most part, the FHA has chosen to encourage and extend rigid race and class segregation.[15] Its underwriting manual of 1938 declared that "if a neighborhood is to retain stability, it is necessary that properties shall continue to be occupied by the same social and racial groups." The FHA composed and distributed a model racially restrictive covenant prohibiting "the occupancy of properties except by the race for which they are intended."

The white suburban movement of the postwar years was

largely the product of FHA financing. The state was also responsible for the building of public housing projects in the central cities after World War II. Public housing is almost always located in the poorest areas and is most often virtually segregated by race. The United States Commission on Civil Rights reports that of the quarter of a million public housing units built in the nation's twenty-four largest metropolitan areas, only seventy-six have been located outside the central city. The result is not only residential segregation, but de facto segregation of urban public schools as well.[16] It was not until 1962 that John F. Kennedy was to issue an executive order that brought to an end the explicitly segregationist practices of the Federal Housing Administration.

Federal responsibility in the struggle for equal opportunity employment entered a new era on June 25, 1941. In an attempt to prevent a march on Washington by A. Phillip Randolph, the black leader of the segregated pullman porters union, Franklin Roosevelt issued Executive Order #8802, which "reaffirmed the policy of the United States to encourage full participation in the *national defense* [my emphasis] program in the firm belief that the democratic life within the nation can be defended successfully only with the help and support of all groups within its borders."[17]

A five-member Fair Employment Practices Committee (FEPC) was authorized to accept and investigate discrimination complaints, to seek negotiated settlements, and to recommend measures to carry out the provisions of the executive order. Two years later, at the peak of the war effort, Roosevelt extended coverage of his executive order to all federal contracts and subcontracts. The Fair Employment Practices Committee concluded in its final report (1947) that its effect had been positive, since blacks had comprised only 3 percent of workers in war industries in 1942, and this had increased to 8 percent by 1945.

Ironically, this federal program covered just those years when affirmative action was least necessary because the unemployment rate was reduced to 1.2 percent at the peak of the war effort. The committee noted in its final report that the gains made by minority groups began to be dissipated as soon as the wartime controls were relaxed and frictional unemployment again became a problem in the transition to a peacetime economy.

The executive order program was at a virtual standstill between 1946 and 1951 since a coalition of Republicans and Southern Democrats refused to permit the expenditures of funds for its implementation. But as the Korean conflict escalated, President Truman followed the example of FDR by issuing executive orders in February and December of 1951 that required defense contractors to promise nondiscrimination on the basis of race, creed, color, or national origin. Once again, the federal government acted at a time when the nature of the labor market (unemployment fell to 2.7 percent by 1952) should have made such an order less essential.

Generally speaking, the pre-1948 period was one in which blacks and women constituted a "reserve army" to be used whenever the nation's security was threatened. When the emergency was over, blacks and women became either invisible, subject to derision, or were put back in their place.

4

The Steady Breakdown of Segregation and Discrimination by the State After 1948

President Truman's order of July 26, 1948, which set up a President's Committee on Equality of Treatment and Opportunity in the Armed Services, was only a politically inspired first step toward desegregation of the armed services, as explained in Chapter 2. The Fahy Committee (1949) succeeded in introducing civilian views on integration into the military, although not without some resistance from Army Secretary Kenneth C. Royall, who, in a statement before the committee in March 1949, was still arguing that the army was "not an instrument for social evolution."[1]

Secretary of Defense Louis Johnson ultimately implemented the end of segregation in the army during the Korean conflict. By the end of the Korean War, few all-black troops remained, and the number of black officers had sharply increased.[2] The military was actually in the vanguard of the Civil Rights movement, integrating its schools prior to the 1954 Supreme Court decision ending "separate but equal" education.[3]

In the years since the Korean War, the armed services have provided a good example of the advantages of full employment and a sellers' market for those who are victims of discrimination. The proportion of blacks in the armed services exceeds the proportion of blacks in the general population, despite the fact that entry requirements for blacks are now somewhat higher than those for whites.[4] By the mid-eighties, blacks constituted 13 percent of all navy personnel, 17 percent of the air force, and 30 percent of the United States Army—in all, about one-fifth of the 2.1 million persons in the armed forces. Ten percent of all army officers are black, as are 7 percent of all generals. A striking 42 percent of all enlisted women are black, and there are a number of black women generals.

The reenlistment rate for blacks is two to three times higher than that for whites. It is clear that the armed services represent a superior way of life for many risk-avoiding blacks as compared with other areas of our society, particularly the free market sector. During the Vietnam War, blacks constituted 20 percent of the front-line troops and suffered 12.1 percent of all American casualties in Southeast Asia.[5] It was therefore entirely fitting that the alternative memorial statue to Vietnam veterans in Washington should include a black among the three soldiers represented.

An important landmark in the breakdown of school segregation was provided by the United States Supreme Court's decision in *Brown v. Board of Education* (1954). The Warren Court's ruling signaled the beginning of the end of the official caste system in the South.[6] Subsequently, the courts have ordered and supported the busing of students in order to bring about a certain amount of racial integration in the school system.

In addition to this momentous decision by the Warren Court, subsequent Supreme Court decisions have brought about a less discriminatory policy with respect to the death penalty. In the postwar years, lynchings of blacks declined markedly, and legal execution of blacks became more common.[7] The fact that a much higher proportion of blacks than whites were being executed led the Supreme Court to decree a moratorium on all executions for a decade, beginning in 1966. A Supreme Court ruling ten years later once again permitted capital punishment under certain loosely defined conditions. Since then, southern states have adjusted their judicial procedures. Between December 14, 1983 and December 13, 1984, twenty-two prisoners were executed—all in the South. Of these, nine were black.[8] Considering the higher percentage of blacks living in the South and the higher black crime rate—particularly the homicide rate—this percentage is thus far apparently low enough not to violate the Eighth Amendment prohibiting "cruel and unusual punishment."[9]

The Eisenhower administration deserves some credit for taking the first affirmative action position in peacetime. In early 1948, General Eisenhower had supported the continuation of segregation in the armed forces, but in 1952 he ran for the presidency on a platform which called for a continuation of the desegregation of the army. In August 1953, after the Korean War, President Eisenhower issued Executive Order #10479, establishing a 15-member Committee on Government Contracts chaired by his vice-president, Richard Nixon. This order reaffirmed the United States policy of promoting equal employment opportunity under government contracts because all persons are "entitled to fair and equitable treatment in all aspects of employment on work paid for from public funds." The following year, upon the recommendation of the Committee on Government Contracts, Eisenhower issued a new order to better explain the nondiscriminatory provision of government contracts and specified that the text of the provision be included in government contracts and subcontracts.

During the Eisenhower years, African leaders from newly independent states were subjected to humiliating treatment during visits to the United States. In one of the most notorious cases, K. A. Gbedeman, Ghana's Foreign Minister, was ill-treated by a white employee in a Howard Johnson's restaurant, not in the South, but in Dover, Delaware. As a result, President Eisenhower and Vice-President Nixon moved swiftly to make amends, which included the revival of a plan to finance a dam and smelter on the Volta River. According to a military historian, "the nation's elected leaders were becoming aware that racism, as practiced here, had a harmful effect among Asian and African states that formed the ideological battleground between the United States and the Soviet Union."[10]

Although Eisenhower's term was an eight-year period of sluggish economic growth in relation to both the Truman and the Kennedy years, the Committee on Government Contracts often attempted to foster minority employment by urging the hiring of blacks on a limited "preferential" basis, i.e., giving preference to a black applicant when a black and white applicant were equally qualified. Generally speaking, the contracting agencies were unwilling to adopt the "firmer approach" of affirmative action recommended by Chairman Nixon. In its final report to President Eisenhower, the committee determined that overt discrimination was not as prevalent as was generally believed. More importantly, it noted "the indifference of employers to establishing a positive policy of nondiscrimination." It remained the task of the Democrats to overcome this indifference.

In March 1961, shortly after entering office, President Kennedy issued Executive Order #10925 establishing the President's Committee on Fair Employment Practices and ordered that federal contractors be required to pledge nondiscrimination and "to take affirmative action to ensure" equal employment opportunity regardless of race, creed, color, or national origin. It should be noted that another decade would go by before the women's liberation movement would be responsible for adding "sex" to the list of those affected by discriminatory practices. President Kennedy's order stated that "it is the general interest and welfare of the United States to promote its economy, security, and *national defense* [my emphasis] through the most efficient and effective utilization of all available manpower." For the first time, the Kennedy order set out strong and specific penalties for noncompliance. Once again, the nation's defense was being utilized as a rationale for opening up opportunities for minorities.

Within a year of the dramatic civil rights march on Washington led by Dr. Martin Luther King, Jr., the United States Congress passed its first comprehensive response to the problem of employment and discrimination: Title VII of the Civil Rights Act of 1964. This act extended the obligation of nondiscrimination to *private* employers who are *not* government contractors, and to unions and employment agencies as well. In 1965, President Johnson's Compliance Activities Committee began a long struggle to break down union barriers in the construction industry, where union traditions of nepotism and overt racial discrimination had virtually excluded minorities from employment on government contracts.

The early 1970s constituted a momentous period for affirmative action in employment. In 1972, Congress passed comprehensive amendments to Title VII of the Civil Rights Act of 1964, expanding coverage to include federal, state, and local employment, and for the first time authorized civil suits by the Equal Employment Opportunity Commission (EEOC). That same year, Congress expanded the coverage of affirmative action policy to include employees in the Civil Service. Targets for affirmative action programs would henceforth include women, disabled veterans, veterans of the Vietnam War, and handicapped persons.

The EEOC and Department of Justice began to seek affirmative action remedies in the courts. Two landmark consent decrees—the cases against American Telephone and Telegraph and the steel industry—reflected the tangible results of government efforts.[11] By the end of the 1970s, affirmative action, including race- and sex-conscious numerical targets, had been endorsed and advanced by each of the three branches of government.

The steady growth in acceptance of affirmative action has not been achieved without some backlash. Among the most prominent opponents of affirmative action have been the neoconservatives, who persist in confusing affirmative action targets with "quotas." Quotas limit the number of persons in certain professions, while targets, or goals, are flexible and in no way limit the numbers in any profession or occupation. Many of those who persist in using the term "quotas" in their opposition to affirmative action were themselves victimized by limiting quotas in the past. At one time during the postwar years, there was a percentage limit to the number of Jewish students accepted in United States medical schools. As a result, many Jewish young people were forced to seek medical education abroad.[12]

It is charged that race- and sex-conscious remedies such as goals, timetables, and ratios constitute "reverse discrimination," or preferential treatment. Many believe that these policies are unfair to white males; that they benefit some who do not need assistance, while failing to help others who do; that they impose undue bureaucratic burdens on employers; and that they threaten standards of merit ingrained in United States society.[13]

It is true that affirmative action plans may result in disappointing the *expectations* of white male workers. To the extent that the implementation of affirmative action may have temporarily disadvantaged white males in relationship to their counterparts of an earlier era, such disadvantage is the inevitable result of compensation for the advantages white males have heretofore enjoyed in the labor force. At the same time, craft unions, which formerly restricted membership to male relatives of members, have been opened up to *all* workers. The former height and weight requirements, which have been invalidated under EEOC law for their exclusion of Hispanics and women, also excluded some white males.[14]

Both critics and defenders of race- and sex-conscious remedies no doubt share the ideal of a society in which sex and skin color have no bearing on opportunity in employment and in society as a whole. Defenders of affirmative action believe that the race- and sex-conscious stage will be needed for some time if the ultimate goal is ever to be realized.

In the eighties, the Reagan Administration attempted to undermine affirmative action by failing to enforce laws and policies developed by preceding Republican and Democratic administrations and upheld by the courts. President Reagan packed the United States Commission on Civil Rights with members who were against affirmative action. In addition, he appointed William Bradford Reynolds to be his chief in the Justice Department's Civil Rights Division. Reynolds characterized affirmative action as a "racial spoils system" that violated the basic American concept of fair play. If this writer's overall hypothesis has any validity, we would expect the efforts by the Reagan Administration to undermine affirmative action to be fruitless.[15]

There is considerable evidence of improvement in the job market for *some* minorities and women. According to an unreleased study of the Office of Federal Contract Compliance Programs (OFCCP) in 1983, minorities and women made greater gains in employment at those establishments contracting with the federal government than at noncontractor companies. A review of over twenty million employees in seventy thousand companies found minority employment to have increased by 20.1 percent and female employment by 15.2 percent between 1974 and 1980, despite total employment growth of only 3 percent. These figures applied to federal contractors. For noncontracting companies, minority employment increased by 12.3 percent and female employment by 2.2 percent, compared with an 8.2 percent growth in total employment over the same period. Among contractors, numbers of black and female officials rose by 96 percent and 73 percent, respectively, while among noncontractors, it was by only 50 and 36 percent.

Some women have benefited significantly as a result of affirmative action programs in the 1970s and 1980s. Formerly male preserves appear to be accepting more female employees, although probably at lower levels. Sixty-five percent of all insurance adjusters and examiners are now women, compared with 27 percent in 1970.[16] During the last decade, the number of bartenders rose by about 130,000; 100,000 of these openings were filled by women. By 1986, 44 percent of all bartenders were women. Between 1960 and 1983, the percentage of men in advertising fell from 86 to 52 percent; in banking and financial management, the percentage went down from 91 to 61 percent. Between 1960 and 1982, the proportion of women engineers rose from 1 to 6 percent; mail carriers from 3 to 17 percent; butchers from 4 to 16 percent; physicians from 6 to 15 percent; and bus drivers from 12 to 50 percent by 1986. In the race for a college diploma, women have been encouraged by the opening up of many professional careers that were formerly dominated by men so that they now account for 52 percent of all undergraduate enrollments.

Women have been particularly successful in penetrating the legal profession, more so than blacks or Hispanics. Women constituted 41 percent of entering law students in 1986, up from 20 percent in 1973 and 4 percent in 1963. They received 38 percent of all law degrees in 1986. Blacks, on the other hand, comprised only 5.4 percent of all first year enrollments in 1986, up slightly from 4.7 percent in 1971. Hispanics went from 1.5 to 3.7 percent of new law students between 1971 and 1986. By 1986, 18 percent of all attorneys were women, twice the percentage in 1976.[17]

At the same time, men have entered some fields that were previously dominated by women. Between 1970 and 1980, more than ten thousand men joined the ranks of airline flight attendants. The number of men who worked as telephone operators increased by five thousand, but this was more than counterbalanced by an increase of twenty-one thousand women working as telephone installers, formerly a male bastion.

Black women have generally fared better than black men, partly because they have tended to remain in school and complete their educations.[18] Among black youth, only eighty-five males currently finish high school for every one hundred females. And among blacks currently in college, there are only seventy-one men for every hundred women. While white women now fill 48 percent of professional positions held by whites, black women account for 66 percent of black professionals. The relative success of black women as compared to black men may be related to the high rates of marital breakup and the growth of the female-headed family in the black community. Among white women aged twenty-five to sixty-five, a total of 73 percent have resident husbands, whereas the comparable figure among black women is 44 percent. In numerical terms, the educational gap between whites and blacks has almost closed. The median number of years in school for blacks in 1980 was 12.0 years, only slightly behind the 12.5 years reported for the white adult population. However, there still remains a gap in the quality of education.

Despite the employment gains for both minorities and women as a result of affirmative action, the relative income data are disappointing. Certain educated minorities and women in stable two-earner families have no doubt scored impressive gains. However, those minorities and women with little education, living outside the traditional nuclear family, have lost ground. Thus, *on average*, little progress has been made in closing the overall discrimination gap for blacks and women. What has occurred is an increase in inequality among blacks and other minorities, as well as among women. This polarization has produced an impressive yet superficial veneer of highly successful blacks and women, as well as a large and growing body of lumpen proletariat.[19]

The typical black family continues to earn about 60 percent of the income of the average white family, and the typical woman earns about the same percentage of the average male income. These percentages have fluctuated somewhat, influenced by the nature of the labor market. In the 1960s and early 1970s, the "New Economics" of the Kennedy and Johnson administrations and Vietnam War years produced lower unemployment rates. The gap between black and white family income narrowed somewhat during that period so that in 1969-70 the income of the black family was 61 percent of that of the white family. Since then, it slipped back to 56 percent in 1981. For black males, the picture is somewhat better. Here, the peak year was 1979, when black males earned 65 percent of white male income.[20] Only black females have scored significant gains in the era of affirmative action. From 1960 to 1981, black females increased their income from 62 percent of their white female counterparts to over 90 percent, with a peak of 96 percent in both 1972 and 1980. By 1979, black female income outside the South exceeded the incomes of white females.

There has also been a significant increase in the number of blacks in highly visible, prestigious positions outside of entertainment and professional sports, where blacks had traditionally excelled before affirmative action. Since 1967, when Carl Stokes was elected mayor of Cleveland, blacks have been elected (and reelected) as mayors of over three hundred United States cities, including Los Angeles, Detroit, Chicago, Baltimore, Washington, Philadelphia, Birmingham, Newark, and Atlanta. Blacks have also been appointed to such high levels of the government bureaucracy as Chief United Nations Representative, the presidential cabinet, National Security Adviser (Colin L. Powell), and the Supreme Court. In 1984 and 1988, the presidential candidacy of Jesse Jackson was taken seriously by both the media and the electorate. Women, likewise, have attained prestigious positions outside of entertainment, including professional sports. Since 1970, women have been elected as mayors in San Francisco, Tampa, Houston, Dallas, and San Jose. They have been appointed to the Supreme Court and positions such as Chief United Nations Representative. Geraldine Ferraro's candidacy for vice-president on the Democratic party ticket in 1984 represented a big step for women in national politics.

It should be mentioned that aggregate income data include only those reporting income. By 1980, 15 percent of all black males aged twenty-five to sixty-four were telling the United States Census Bureau that they had earned absolutely nothing in 1979. Because of this low labor force participation rate and higher dependency ratios, black per capita incomes are significantly lower than they would appear to be if we only looked at conventional comparisons. There are also weaknesses in black earnings which show up when we look at different geographical regions. Only in the South—as a result of the one-time only gains associated with the mechanization of cotton production and rural to urban migration—do we find a significant improvement in relative black family income after 1960. Thus, the discrimination gap within the United States appears to be evening out and becoming more uniform.

Some disturbing signs of deteriorating conditions among the black population include the increase in female-headed families, high and rising unemployment rates among the young (2.5 times the white rate), falling labor force participation rates—especially among males—and a rising incidence of violent death and of incarceration in prisons. The new phenomenon of mass homelessness is also disproportionately a black problem. In some cities, over 70 percent of the homeless are African-Americans.[21]

The picture of stalled progress is dramatically clear in higher education. Although the pool of minority high school graduates was becoming bigger and better than ever, minority college attendance rates initially fell and have remained disproportionally low. Between 1975 and 1985, the college participation rate for white youths rose from 53 to 55 percent; for blacks it fell from 48 percent to 44 percent. During the same period, the number of blacks earning Master's degrees declined by 32 percent, and the number earning doctorates fell by 5 percent.[22] The conclusion of a recent report is not reassuring:

> In summary, the economic prospects for black citizens are bleak: almost half of them begin life in poverty; they grow up to face high unemployment rates (over two times higher than that of whites); and in their old age, they are three times more likely than whites to live in poverty.[23]

5

Discrimination in Advanced Capitalist Non-Superpowers

In many respects, Canada would seem to be the most appropriate non-superpower to compare with the United States. Its level of capital accumulation is roughly on a par with that of the United States; its political institutions are not too dissimilar from those of the United States; the governments of both countries are fairly responsive to the wishes of their citizenry; and both lands are inhabited by a mosaic of races and ethnic groups.

Unlike the United States, however, there is no history of black slavery in Canada. Most of the few blacks in Canada emigrated from the United States after the Revolutionary War or, later, from the Caribbean. Like similar immigrants in the United States, they are not particularly deprived.[1] According to Thomas Sowell, Caribbean blacks in the United States have socioeconomic characteristics that are about average for society as a whole.[2] Both Canada and the United States have native Indian populations that are terribly depressed and subject to considerable paternalism on the part of the state.

In the 1980s, Canada's unemployment rate has been 3 to 4 percentage points higher than that of the United States. At the same time, the United States economy—as behooves that of an advanced capitalist superpower—is much more dependent on the spending of its military-industrial complex. Nevertheless, there is a great deal of influence, both economic and cultural, on Canada by the United States, so we would expect to find many institutional similarities.[3]

It is therefore surprising to find this statement in the Abella Report of the Commission on Equality in Employment, dated October 1984:

> The country to which Canada has the closest physical and cultural proximity has had for two decades an intensive program of affirmative action. What was striking was that the American government had, for 20 years, made genuine efforts to rectify obvious employment inequities in the private sector, while Canadians were still considering whether to take any steps at all. To many, this inability or unwillingness in Canada to confront the problem was saddening; to others it was enraging. It is one thing to learn from any mistakes of the American experience; it is another to ignore the experience altogether.[4]

If Canadian women had significantly better opportunities than United States women, we shouldn't be surprised at the comparative lack of affirmative action by our northern neighbor. But, in fact, Canadian statistics on the relative welfare of women are remarkably similar to those in the United States.

Like the United States, the Canadian female labor force has been showing greater growth than the male labor force. Between 1966 and 1982, the male labor force grew by 35.6 percent, the female labor force by 119.4 percent. The female labor force participation rate in the United States increased from 43.3 percent in 1970 to 52.9 percent in 1983; in Canada, the increase was from 37.1 percent in 1971 to 51.6 percent in 1982.[5] Only the Scandinavian countries—Norway, Denmark, Finland, and Sweden—have higher female labor force participation rates among the advanced capitalist countries.

Canadian women are also concentrated in the clerical, sales, and service occupations and are barely represented in engineering and architecture. The situation is better in the newer computer-related occupations, such as systems analysis and computer programming, which has shown the greatest growth among professional female occupations and one of the lowest male-female earnings differentials.

Average female employment income as a percentage of average male employment income is about the same as in the United States. From 1971 to 1982, female income as a percentage of male income rose from 60.6 percent to 63.9 percent. In the United States, the income gap for year-round full-time workers was 64 percent in the mid-fifties; it fell to 58 percent in the mid-sixties and was back to 64 percent by 1985.[6] The only occupations in which women reported an average income exceeding $30,000 per year were medicine, surgery, and dentistry. Even so, women, who accounted for 17 percent of all doctors, averaged income that was only 60 percent of that of their male counterparts.[7] Seventy-seven percent of all women are found in only five of the twenty-two major job categories—those at the bottom of the salary scale.[8]

During the fifties and sixties, Canadian female unemployment rates were below male unemployment rates. Beginning in 1969, however, the relative unemployment rates were reversed until 1982, when the male rate increased sharply in the recession of that year and became higher again than the female rate. In the United States, female unemployment rates have been typically somewhat higher than male unemployment rates, except during recent recessions and in the 1980s, when changes in rates were similar to those of Canada.

The unemployment rates for Canadians of British, Japanese, Korean, Chinese, Pacific Islands, and "other European" ethnic backgrounds are typically lower than the national average, while those for French Canadians, Indo-Chinese, blacks, native peoples, and Latin Americans are above the national average. The unemployment rates were highest for native peoples in 1981: 16.5 percent for males and 17.3 percent for females.

As in the United States, the male-female education gap is closing. Today one-half of university undergraduate degrees are awarded to females, an increase from 38 percent in 1971. Women in Canada earn 39 percent of the M.A. degrees and 24 percent of Canadian Ph.D.s. In the United States, women received about half of all B.A.s and M.A.s and more than one-third of doctoral degrees.[10] Despite the increase in female university students, only 15.5 percent of the full-time teaching staff at Canadian universities in 1980-81 was female. In the United States, on the other hand, women increased as a percentage of college teachers from 19 to 25 percent between 1962 and 1982.[11]

Canada has licensed day-care centers for less than 15 percent of preschool aged children. It appears that significantly more day care is available in the United States than in Canada, although United States facilities fall far short of demand in both quality and quantity. As in the United States, a Wartime Day Nurseries Act provided child care for the increasing numbers of Canadian working mothers during World War II.[12] In 1946, when Canadian and United States fighting men returned home to take jobs, women were encouraged to leave the labor force, and the government-operated day-care centers closed in both countries.

Canadians recognize the difficulty of introducing affirmative action in their faltering economy. The unemployment rate in August 1984 was not expected to improve significantly throughout the balance of the decade. However, in an effort to mobilize support for affirmative action, Canadians cite a United States study which concludes that the United States has enjoyed a 50 percent return on its investment in affirmative action.[13]

As in the United States, some Canadians associate affirmative action with the imposition of quotas. The Royal Commission proposed the term, "employment equity," since the use of "affirmative action" had been a "semantic red flag."[14] Whichever term is used, the intent of the Commission is to open job competition to all who would have been eligible but for the existence of discrimination. In the words of the *Report of the Commission on Equality in Employment* :

> The effect may be to end the hegemony of one group over the economic spoils, but the end of exclusivity is not reverse dis-

crimination, it is the beginning of equality. The economic advancement of women and minorities is not the granting of a privilege or advantage to them; it is the removal of a bias in favor of white men that has operated at the expense of other groups.[15]

Equal pay for work of equal value was written into the law governing the federal public service, the Federal Crown Corporations (such as Air Canada), and federally regulated corporations as early as 1978. However, it has seldom been enforced and only on complaint. Sylvia Gold, the new president of the Canadian Advisory Council on the Status of Women and a member of the New Democratic party appointed by Conservative Prime Minister Brian Mulroney, has recognized the fact that Ottawa will have to exert some muscle to get the private sector to pay men and women the same wages for work of equal value.[16]

Unlike the United States, Canada was one of more than a hundred governments to sign the International Labor Organization's Convention 100 of 1951 requiring "equal remuneration for men and women workers for work of equal *value* [my emphasis]." Governments that ratify this convention must "promote objective appraisal of jobs." This "comparable worth" legislation has resulted in Canada's Human Rights Commission ordering equal value pay for nurses and librarians, among others.[17]

Like the United States Armed Forces, the Canadian Air Force is not a very hospitable place for homosexuals. In 1985, it was reported that five alleged lesbians were dismissed from a base in Shelburne, Nova Scotia. The women were dismissed because their "abnormal sexual activity" was said to pose a risk to national security. Several of these women were oceanographic operators tracking Soviet submarines in the Atlantic. Lesbians claimed that they were not covered by the constitution or the Charter of Rights and Freedom (to be discussed momentarily). Critics of the charter feared that they might be.[18]

In April 1985, the anti-discrimination part of Canada's three-year-old constitution went into effect. Section 15 forbids discrimination on grounds of sex, color, race, ethnic origin, religion, or disability. Section 15 had been repatriated from Great Britain three years earlier when Canada was under the Liberal leadership of Premier Pierre Trudeau. The delay enabled Ottawa and the ten provincial governments to rewrite their laws to make them agree with the charter. Paradoxically, Premier Brian Mulroney of the Progressive Conservative party is presiding over the introduction of employment equity into Canada at the same time that President Ronald Reagan is attempting to water down the United States affirmative action program.[19]

Japan is one of the latest countries to pass an Equal Employment Bill, which was scheduled to take effect in April 1986.[20] After seven years of public debate and behind-the-scenes compromise, the Japanese Parliament passed a bill encouraging employers to end discrimination on the basis of sex in their hiring, assignment, and promotion policies. Severe limits on overtime and late-night work, which have kept women out of many jobs, will be ended. There are no penalties for employers who continue discrimination. It is suspected that international pressure—particularly the United Nations "Decade for Women," which ended in the summer of 1985—accelerated movement by the Japanese Parliament. This law was necessary in order for Japan to ratify the United Nations Convention banning sexual discrimination.

Japanese women make up 35 percent of the labor force but only 6 percent of managerial positions. Overall, their salaries are less than 50 percent of those paid to men. In 1984, for the first time, more than half of all married women held jobs. As in the United States, it is expected that want ads specifying the sex of the applicant will be eliminated. The Japanese female labor force participation rate has been stagnating for some time, and, as I observed in 1977, women working in department stores were being urged to give up their jobs to men. Only 22.9 percent of all university students were female in 1983–84.[21]

British women have benefited somewhat from job-bias laws such as the Equal Pay Act of 1975. As a result, women's wages as a percentage of men's rose from 56 percent in 1970 to 67 percent in 1981, although they had slipped back to 66 percent by 1986. Only 5.8 percent of Britain's managerial jobs are held by women—roughly the same as in Japan. Child-care facilities in the private sector are worse than they are in the United States, and British antidiscrimination laws aren't as tough as those in the United States.[22]

As in the United States and Canada, female labor force participation rates have been rising in most Western European countries, with the exception of the Federal Republic of Germany, Switzerland, and Austria. The decline in West Germany has been rather significant and contrasts sharply with developments in the German Democratic Republic. There is now a 32 percentage point difference between the female labor force participation rates of the two Germanies.

In the last decade, the greatest increases in female labor force participation rates have been in the Netherlands, Norway, Italy, Canada, and the United States, in that order. For complete data, see Table 2, which also includes selected socialist countries to be discussed in Chapter 7. Since socialist female labor force participation rates were already high in 1975, the percentage increases have been smaller in Eastern Europe. The German Democratic Republic has continued to increase significantly the participation of female workers, even in relation to other socialist countries. In 1984, the GDR's rate slightly exceeded that of Sweden's.[23]

Sylvia Hewlett has argued less than convincingly that Western European women are more liberated than United States women because of their better provisions for child-care.[24] The greater development of government child-care facilities in Western Europe may reflect competition with nearby Eastern European countries where, as we shall see, child-care facilities are even more advanced. It is especially difficult to accept Hewlett's appreciation of the status of West German women, in

Table 2

The Economic Role of Women in the ECE Region and in North America, 1975 to 1985

Country	Labor force participation rates for females (labor force as percentage of population, ages 15 to 64) 1975	1985	Changes in female labor force partic-ipation rates: 1985 as % of 1975
Austria	53.6	53.1	99.1
Belgium	43.9	49.3	112.3
Denmark	63.5	73.6	115.9
Finland	65.5	73.8	112.7
France	49.9	51.7	103.6
West Germany	49.6	45.1	90.9
Ireland	33.4	36.5	109.3
Italy	34.6	42.3	122.2
Netherlands	33.1	42.9	129.6
Norway	53.3	68.5	128.5
Sweden	67.6	77.3	114.3
Switzerland	49.6	48.3	97.4
United Kingdom	55.4	59.9	108.1
Canada	50.0	60.9	121.8
United States	53.2	64.8	121.8
Czechoslovakia	66.6	68.0	102.1
East Germany	71.5	77.5	108.4
Hungary	61.9	63.0	101.8
USSR	68.6	70.0	102.0

Source: United Nations, *The Economic Role of Women in the ECE Region, Developments, 1975/85* (New York, 1985), 14.

view of the declining female labor force participation rates there.

One measure of the status of women is their representation in the parliaments of the advanced capitalist countries. Here, the Scandinavian countries do the best in the West, with women holding about 25 percent of the seats. In France, women hold less than 6 percent of the seats. France ranks fourteenth among Western European countries when it comes to female representation in parliament, running behind such conservative countries as Italy and Ireland.[25] In Great Britain, only 4.2 percent of the members of parliament are women, despite the fact that their Prime Minister is "Iron Lady" Margaret Thatcher.[26] In the United States, the figure for women in Congress is 4.7 percent, very slightly above the 4.5 percent of Congress members who are black.

The United States and Canada are far ahead of Great Britain and the Federal Republic of Germany in providing a positive climate for minority business development. England still believes that its ethnic population will one day "go back home," while the Federal Republic of Germany does not recognize its immigrants as being German. The French didn't establish a national minority business program until 1985, after studying the United States model of MBDA which dates back to the Office of Minority Business Enterprise created in 1969.[27]

Generally speaking, the United States and Canada offer the best opportunities for women and nonwhites with the possible exception of the Scandinavian countries. Of the two North American countries, the United States seems to be somewhat more advanced in its treatment of women and racial minorities.

6

Affirmative Action and Environmental Policy in the USSR Since the Revolution

Economic and Political Discrimination

Since its inception, the Soviet Union has pursued a domestic policy which encourages both racial and sexual equality. In its foreign policy, the USSR typically supports the oppressed rather than the capitalist ruling classes abroad, the less developed areas rather than the advanced capitalist countries.[1] As a result, countries and groups that are subject to political pressure from the United States have frequently relied on the Soviets for assistance.[2] The Soviet economic philosophy, which puts a higher priority on abolishing absolute poverty, homelessness, begging, etc., has served as an example for those countries following that philosophy. In the words of the only black Nobel Laureate in Economics, W. Arthur Lewis:

> It is to the credit of Marxist-inspired societies that abolition of absolute poverty is among their first priorities, and there is no reason why rich capitalist societies, inspired by religious ideals, should lag in this respect.[3]

Lewis echoes a theme discussed by Gunnar Myrdal in *An American Dilemma*:

> Myrdal asserted that white Americans experienced a troubling dilemma because of the discrepancy between the hallowed

"American Creed," whereby they think, talk, and act under the influence of egalitarian and Christian principles, and the oppressive way they treated Afro-Americans.[4]

From the beginning, the Soviet state has always regarded racial discrimination as a crime. The first Soviet constitution, passed in 1918, said: "The Russian Socialist Federation Soviet Republic,[5] recognizing the equal rights of citizens irrespective of their racial and national origin, declares as running against the basic laws of the Republic establishment or tolerance of any privileges or advantages on these grounds as well as any oppression of national minorities or limitation of their equal rights." In addition to abolishing racial and national discrimination, the constitution gave equal rights to women. These principles are also recorded in the fourth and latest constitution of 1977, which states:

> Citizens of the USSR of different races and nationalities have equal rights. Exercise of these rights is ensured by a policy of all-round development and drawing together of all the nations and nationalities of the USSR, by educating citizens in the spirit of Soviet patriotism and socialist internationalism, and by the possibility to use their native language and the languages of other peoples of the USSR. Any direct or indirect limitation of the rights of citizens or establishment of direct or indirect privileges on the grounds of race or nationality and any advocacy of racial or national exclusiveness, hostility or contempt, are punishable by law.

In 1965, the United Nations passed a convention on the elimination of all forms of racial discrimination. The convention states that the ideology and policy of racism constitute a crying contradiction of international law and that it is the duty of all states to guarantee the equality of all of their citizens before the law, regardless of race, skin color, or national and ethnic origin. Since 1968, when the convention came into force, it has been signed by 120 countries. The USSR was the first great power to ratify the convention. Unfortunately, the United

States has yet to ratify this United Nations convention, just as it failed for thirty-seven years to sign an earlier convention against genocide.[6]

The USSR has consistently supported United Nations decisions to isolate and boycott the Union of South Africa. The USSR has also insisted on the "unconditional fulfillment of the resolutions passed by the Organization of African Unity and other international organizations demanding the abolition of apartheid and any other forms of racial discrimination, and advocating the right of the people of Namibia to shape their own future and the right for the South African black majority to enjoy peace and freedom."[7]

The United States, on the other hand, has tried to use its influence, especially the investment of its multinational corporations, to allow gradually for greater democracy and economic welfare for blacks in South Africa. As suggested in Chapter 2, segregation is counterproductive when it comes to the maximization of profits. Thus, it has not been too difficult for most progressive, profit-minded multinationals based in the United States to subscribe to the so-called "Sullivan Principles." Nevertheless, beginning in 1986 it became increasingly clear that many United States citizens—particularly the black civil rights activists (including the Reverend Sullivan himself in June 1987)—were becoming impatient with President Reagan's approach of "constructive engagement" with the Pretoria regime. Even conservative Republicans, like Representative Newt Gingrich of Georgia, were calling for an end to apartheid in recent years.

In practice, Soviet affirmative action is most striking in predominantly nonwhite Central Asia. At the time of the revolution, this area was extremely poor and had scarcely been integrated into the Czarist Empire. These republics (Kazakhstan, Uzbekistan, Turkmenia, Tazikistan, and Kir-ghizia) have typically been developing at a more rapid rate than other republics, particularly the RSFSR, or Russian Republic. In the words of Michael Ellman:

> Soviet regional policy combines both large-scale industrial in-
> vestment and rapid expansion of social services such as educa-
> tion and medical care in densely populated, formerly backward
> areas, such as Central Asia, with large-scale natural resource
> development in sparsely populated Siberia. The enormous ex-
> pansion of urban employment opportunities in Soviet Central
> Asia during the period of Soviet power is a major achieve-
> ment of Soviet power.[8]

In the 1930s, when Stalin was ostensibly exacting a "tribute"
from agriculture through low procurement prices for compulsory deliveries, the procurement price for cotton—a principal crop produced in Central Asia—was much higher relative to
its costs of production than were those for other agricultural
products.[9] The rapid development of the Central Asian region
can be explained by the fact that turnover taxes collected in the
region are used to finance local development rather than military and international expenditures. This is not the case with a
large share of the turnover taxes collected in the Russian Republic. According to Gertrude E. Schroeder: "In sum, it appears that considerable redistribution of income among the
republics has taken place in the Soviet period, with the Central
Asian Republics the principal gainers and also perhaps Georgia
and Armenia (until recently)."[10]

Before the Russian Revolution, Jews had been legally barred
from government service and from work on the railroads and in
the postal services.[11] After the revolution, these laws were
simply wiped off the books. Affirmative action placed 150,000
Jews in industrial jobs in the 1920s, before unemployment was
officially eliminated during the First Five-Year Plan.[12] With the
organization of state farms, the proportion of Jews earning a
living in agriculture rose from 2 to 11 percent in the years before World War II. Anti-Semitic quotas in education were
abolished, and the possibility of education in one's native language was provided everywhere.

Tatars, Gypsies, and numerous other dispersed minorities

had similar experiences, although discrimination against them was less firmly fixed in Czarist law. According to William Mandel, "the Tatars overcame the heritage of their former depressed status in a single generation or at most two; with the Gypsies it took two generations for most, for some three."

World War II undid the settling of Soviet Gypsies, some of whom had been organized as collective farmers. With the advancement of Nazi troops, the Gypsies, who had been targeted for extinction by Hitler, naturally dispersed. During the war, Gypsies fought in the Soviet Army and as partisans. After World War II, roving bands of Gypsies created problems for the non-Gypsy populace, eventually necessitating a decree dated October 5, 1956, "On Reconciling Vagrant Gypsies to Labor."

According to the 1979 census, there are over 209,000 Gypsies within the USSR, up slightly from the 1959 census, and it is believed that large numbers of other Soviet citizens have some Gypsy blood. In the early years of the new revolutionary government, intermarriages of Russian Bolsheviks with Gypsies and Jews was considered a positive "political act." Gypsies have their own theater in Moscow (founded in 1931) and are found in most of the arts. However, it is obvious to any frequent traveler in the USSR that there is still a scattering of mobile Gypsies outside the planning sector engaged in hawking and fortune-telling.

During World War II, some of the ethnic groups supposedly collaborated with the invading Germans and were subsequently deported to the east. These were the Crimean Tatars, Volga Germans, Miskhetians, Kalmyks, and four nationalities of the Northern Caucasus: Chechins, Ingush, Balkars, and Karachai. To this day, some of these groups (the Volga Germans, Crimean Tatars, and Miskhetians) are restricted from living in their former homelands.[13] This position has apparently been taken because of the traumatic Soviet experiences of World War II rather than racial prejudice, since the Volga Germans are Caucasian.

Women in the Soviet Union have also been subjected to liberation from above since 1917. They almost immediately received the right to vote (a pioneer right for women at this time); the right to inexpensive, easy divorce; the right to hold jobs that had formerly been reserved almost exclusively for men; and, in 1920, the right to inexpensive abortion.[14] As early as 1923, over half of the Soviet university students specializing in medicine and the arts were women, and women generally constituted 43 percent of all university students.[15]

The right to free or inexpensive abortions was suspended for twenty years (1936–1956), thus preceding the 1937 unpublished census which shocked Stalin with its low initial count.[16] After its legalization again in 1956, abortion came to be used as a form of birth control. Today's Soviet woman undergoes an average of three abortions in her lifetime. The average is probably much higher in Moscow and Leningrad since this practice is negligible in Central Asia.[17] The poor quality and frequent unavailability of both sex education and contraceptives are apparently at the root of this continuing problem.

Divorce laws were also tightened during approximately the same twenty-year period when abortion was illegal and, especially after 1944, as a result of astronomical wartime population losses. Subsequently—in particular, since the relative liberalization beginning in 1956—the Soviet Union has become second in the world in the percentage of marriages ending in divorce, the United States being the leader.[18] Hewlett has correctly pointed out the negative impact of divorce on the welfare of United States women and children when 60 percent of divorced fathers fail to support their children. Automatic deductions of child support from Soviet fathers' pay greatly reduces, if not eliminates, this problem in the USSR. Obviously, there is nothing to prevent Soviet divorced fathers from taking menial low-paying jobs where deductions of one-third of the salary are inadequate for child support.

The labor force participation rates of Soviet women are slightly lower than those for women in the German Democratic

Republic due to the negative influence of Central Asia on the average. Women in the Soviet Union are more typically found in occupations which are dominated by men in the advanced capitalist system. This is particularly true in such areas as engineering (one-third of the total as compared with 6 percent in the United States), veterinary science, and architecture. Soviet women also more frequently pilot passenger planes and occupy outer space at an earlier stage of development than non-Soviet women. However, by 1983 women occupied only 11 percent of industrial management posts, up 2 percentage points per decade. They also account for a mere 13 percent of those holding doctorates of science.[19] Their presence is lacking chiefly in high political offices, such as the Politburo. Only 3 percent of the Central Committee members and 9 percent of the Academy of Sciences members are women.[20] However, at the prestigious Institute for the Study of the U.S. and Canada, a relatively new institute, about one-third of the professionals are women.

Until the 27th Party Congress in 1986—and the election of Alexandra P. Biryukova as secretary of the CPSU Central Committee (later promoted to the Politburo in October 1988)—only one woman, Ekaterina Furtseva, was a member of the Politburo, and she was eventually forced to resign as a result of the disclosure that she had spent over one hundred thousand rubles on her dacha. Albert Szymanski's conclusion is that "women are in a far better position at the local and intermediate levels of the political structure in the USSR than they are in the United States, but are very rare at the very top levels in either country."[21]

In relation to capitalist countries and even the German Democratic Republic, the USSR's gross enrollment percentage of women aged fifteen to sixty-four in institutions of higher education is a low 23 percent, compared with 34 percent in Canada.[22] However, the proportion of women in science, engineering, and medicine is probably the highest in the world at approximately 48 percent, compared with 43 percent in the German Democratic Republic and 22 percent in Hungary and Canada. Because of lagging Central Asia, women still constitute less than half of all persons with tertiary level education. But the greatest gains relative to men since 1939 have been made precisely in Central Asia, as well as in the Baltic Republics, where prewar bourgeois societies were to some extent critical of working women.[23]

Data on Soviet women's wages relative to men's wages are considered restricted information by Soviet authorities. One early Western estimate has put them as high as 80 percent of men's wages, which the author now concedes to be on the high side.[24] There is still much crowding of women into such low-paying occupations as nursery and preschool teaching, nursing, and even medicine, in which incomes are only about average for the country as a whole despite the prestigious status of the profession. Men in medicine more frequently serve as higher-paid surgeons and administrators. While women do direct factories (as mentioned above), as well as state and collective farms, they are less likely than men to hold top administrative jobs. Albert Szymanski concludes:

> Compared to their position in the professions, Soviet women have been less successful in attaining administrative positions, but considered in relation to their earlier position in Russian society and to that of women in the West (both in countries at similar levels of economic development and such highly advanced countries as the U.S.A.), they have done very well.[25]

Soviet women are also subject to affirmative action by not being eligible for the draft (which would entail serving their country for two or three years at very low pay). They may also retire (or begin to draw their pensions) five years earlier than men—at age fifty-five rather than at sixty in most occupations.[26]

The darker side of this picture is the behavior of Soviet men in the home. Like Western men, they are reluctant to increase their contribution to domestic life in such activities as cleaning, cooking, and shopping.[27] Since shopping has usually been a time-consuming, difficult task under Soviet conditions, this failure of men has brought about the usual "second shift" for employed women. It has been estimated that women perform approximately two-thirds of all housework and child rearing.[28] Younger men seem to be more responsive in this area, and it is not uncommon to see young men pushing baby carriages in the streets and parks. The low birth rates in the RSFSR and in the Baltic Republics are indicative of greater influence of women in these areas on the size of their families. Large families and "Mother Heroines" in Central Asia, Georgia, Azerbaijan, and Armenia are illustrative of the fact that these women still have a way to go before social equality has been achieved. There are reports of the continuation of the "bride price" in Central Asia. In 1988, there were over thirty cases of self-immolation among young Tadjik women. In this Republic, the birthrate of 6.3 per family is the highest in the USSR.[29] Nevertheless, there are signs that the birth rate has already fallen by one-half in Central Asian urban areas—from a median family of ten to one of five.

Soviet treatment of homosexuals still leaves a great deal to be desired. The Leninist Soviet Union was very tolerant of homosexuality in the twenties, a time when there was a great deal of experimentation in the arts. Homosexual acts between consenting male adults only became illegal in early 1934.[30] To this day, some of these acts are punishable by five years' imprisonment. A highly publicized case occurred in 1974, when the celebrated Georgian movie director, Sergei Paradzhanov, was sentenced to six years' imprisonment for practicing homosexuality and incitement to suicide.[31]

Historically, there has been extensive discrimination in the USSR on both religious and political grounds. Religious persecution and the pursuit of atheistic educational policies by the state were especially great before World War II and, particularly, after a resolution of April 8, 1929, "On Religious Cults." Stalin needed support from the Orthodox Church to defeat the Nazis in World War II and therefore relented somewhat in his pursuit of atheism. Subsequently, the Russian Orthodox Church has enjoyed a privileged position relative to the Catholics and the Baptists. Fundamentalist sects such as Evangelical Christian Baptists, Pentecostals, and True and Free Seventh-Day Adventists, who have traditionally defied state power by refusing to be drafted and insisting on religious education for their children, are still subject to extreme discrimination.[32] There was some increase in the persecution of religious believers during the Khrushchev years, although this appears to have been only a temporary regression.[33]

Political discrimination has characterized Soviet history from the beginning. In the early years, persons with bourgeois backgrounds were barred from higher education. Promotion to positions of authority has been easier for members of the Communist party, although it is claimed that greater work effort is also required from exemplary party members. More recently, employment discrimination has affected Jewish "refuseniks," those who apply for emigration but are turned down for various reasons. Admission to universities in the Western Ukraine was limited to no more than 25 percent of the local Ukrainian population, in accordance with secret instructions in 1974.[34]

Soviet Environmental Policy in a NFL Economy

In the 1970s, when I first began to think about Soviet environmental policy, it seemed to me that President Nixon had triggered a change in Soviet environmental attitudes when he declared "Earth Day" in the Spring of 1970. Later, the 1973 Soviet campaign to clean up the air in Moscow seemed to be a direct reaction to the earlier efforts of New York City to improve its air quality. One of my students, Bob Kirsch, did considerable research on this topic and convinced me that Soviet initiatives, particularly those related to the pollution of Lake Baikal, preceded President Nixon's declaration. William Mandel also argues that the big change in Soviet environmental policy occurred in 1966 and coincided with a special issue of

Soviet Life devoted to the problem. Two years later, a Land Law came into effect, protecting some state and collective farm land from industrial expansion.[35] Thus, a case can only be made for interaction between the two environmental movements on the part of the superpowers, and it is difficult to support my original position which held that there have been special United States initiatives in this respect.

According to Soviet legend, the first Soviet environmental laws encouraging conservation were passed after Lenin was appalled by the cutting of trees in Sokolniki Park in Moscow. Stumpage fees were decreed at an early stage, aimed at the Soviet exploitation of timber, with high fees levied in the European part of the USSR to discourage lumbering there rather than in Siberia. Nevertheless, as in the case of the United States during the nineteenth century, the developmental pressures for exploitation of more easily accessible timber have tended to take precedence over conservation legislation such as stumpage fees.[36]

As compared with the United States, there has been a bias *against* petroleum and *in favor of* coal as an energy source throughout Soviet economic history. Turnover taxes were levied on petroleum products as early as 1930. The coal industry, which produces more pollution, has most frequently been subsidized by the state budget. Soviet planners have consistently underestimated the success of Soviet prospectors in finding oil and natural gas. This was most apparent in Stalin's time when the perspective plan for 1960, which was announced in early 1946, projected a long-term goal of only sixty million tons, far less than what was actually achieved by that date. For many years, Western sovietologists criticized the "backwardness" of the Soviet energy fuel mix; however, there has been less criticism since OPEC escalated world oil prices in November 1973.

Soviet worries over the pollution of Lake Baikal can be traced back to 1963, although remedies for this situation came in the 1970s.[37] Soviet budget announcements at the end of each year now indicate special allocations for the environment, and these have been increasing rapidly. From 1981 to 1986, annual environmental allocations have grown from six to ten billion rubles.[38] As Premier Brezhnev recognized in connection with the draft guidelines of Plan XI at the 26th Party Congress in 1981, such expenditures tend to cut down on overall growth rates in a NFL economy. On the other hand, in the United States FL economy since World War II, such expenditures create employment and profits for firms engaged in cleaning up the environment (see item 10 of Table 1).

Grass roots initiatives aimed at cleaning up the Soviet environment are apparently encouraged by the Soviet State.[39] Article 18 of the 1977 constitution recognized the present generation's responsibility toward future generations: "In the interests of the present and future generations, the necessary steps are taken in the USSR to protect and make scientific, rational use of the land and its mineral and water resources, and the plant and animal kingdoms, to preserve the purity of air and water, ensure reproduction of national wealth, and improve the human environment." Finally, Article 67 states that "citizens are obligated to protect nature and conserve its riches."

Soviet advocates of nuclear power (before Chernobyl, at least) frequently argued that the use of nuclear energy would cause less pollution of the environment than coal and oil. In general, there is an inordinate amount of worship of science and technology in the USSR, as well as great reverence for the technological superiority of the United States.[40]

The environmental movement in the smaller Eastern European countries is much less advanced than it is in the USSR. There would appear to be a greater need for such a movement due to less control over the use of private automobiles, particularly those produced in the German Democratic Republic (Trabant and Wartburg), which are especially polluting.[41]

In Hungary in 1985, white buttons with a broken blue line symbolizing the Danube were worn by those protesting the construction of a dam on the border between Czechoslovakia and Hungary. In addition, six thousand signatures of protest were obtained from those concerned about the environmental impact of the dam. In contrast to the United States and many other advanced capitalist countries, there has been virtually no opposition to the building of nuclear power plants in any of the socialist countries. One exception to this in the West is France, where, like the USSR, nuclear waste is vitrified.[42]

Military Spending in a NFL Environment

Just as competition with the United States has apparently tended to accelerate Soviet environmental expenditures, United States spending on the military-industrial complex and foreign aid has usually produced increases in Soviet arms expenditures and promises of military aid to the Third World, beginning in the Khrushchev era. An obvious example of this interaction occurred in 1961 after Premier Khrushchev's confrontation with John F. Kennedy in Vienna. President Kennedy returned to Washington and asked Congress to help him make good on his campaign promise to rectify the eight years of Eisenhower austerity for the armed forces, which included closing the so-called "missile gap." Later, on July 1, 1961, Khrushchev asked for an unprecedented 44 percent increase in Soviet military expenditures in mid-fiscal year. The effect on both superpowers of this substantial increase in military spending in the first half of the 1960s was dramatic. The United States FL economy embarked on a rapid, long, recession-free expansion at the same time that the Soviet Union's NFL economy slowed down significantly.[43]

During the Reagan years, United States military spending has increased by leaps and bounds, averaging 6 or 7 percent annually in real terms. At the same time, the official Soviet budgetary allocations for defense either remained unchanged or moved downward for about a decade preceding 1985. Even the CIA revised downward its earlier claims about the growth of Soviet defense expenditures, now estimating that the increase after 1976 was less than 2 percent annually. Finally, in November

1984, the Soviets announced a significant 12 percent increase in military spending.[44] If there is anything to the hypothesis that military spending slows down the Soviet NFL economy, we would expect a certain overall sluggishness to ensue should these increases in military spending be real and continue. At the same time, United States military spending in the 1980s, along with an easy fiscal policy, helps explain the superior growth record of the United States FL economy as compared with Japan and the FRG, where fiscal tightness has prevailed.

7

Discrimination and Segregation in Advanced Socialist Non-Superpowers

The importance of discrimination in various socialist economies is presumably related to the nature of the labor market, as well as the level of capital accumulation (capital stock per capita). Socialist Yugoslavia has suffered for some time from double-digit unemployment. It is thus more vulnerable to restrictionist labor policies which exclude women than are other non-capitalist countries which have maintained full or overfull employment conditions. The low level of capital accumulation in Yugoslavia, in addition to the large share of its population still working in agriculture, represents an obstacle to state decisions and institutional development which would favor women and minorities. The fact that there is a rather large Moslem population (principally, but not exclusively, Albanian in Kosovo) also poses some special problems for Yugoslav women.

At the other end of the Eastern European development spectrum, we find the German Democratic Republic, which has suffered from a severe labor shortage during the past forty years. The GDR's female labor force participation rate is the highest in the world since the state provides many positive incentives for women to work outside the home.[1] Good child-care facilities are provided for the lion's share of children over three years of age.[2] The labor force participation rate for women with children between the ages of three and six is 85 percent, compared to 75 percent in Hungary, 48 percent in the United States, and 34 percent in the Federal Republic of Germany.[3]

In addition, the level of capital accumulation in the GDR is the highest (and the share of agricultural activity is the lowest) within the noncapitalist world. Thus, we would expect to find less sexism in the GDR than in the less developed socialist countries, including the USSR, which still has to contend with a relatively large agricultural population and the influence of Islam on the treatment of women in the Central Asian Republics.[4]

Affirmative Action for Women in Hungary

To test the hypothesis that there is more pressure on the superpowers than on the non-superpowers to provide affirmative action for minorities, including women, we shall examine the case of Hungary. Hungary has been a socialist society with more or less full employment, as well as a level of capital accumulation or industrialization that most closely resembles that of the USSR.[5] In particular, we shall look at affirmative action for women and Gypsies in Hungary as compared with the USSR.

Hungary, like all socialist countries, has encouraged women to contribute to the paid labor force. In 1949, nearly two-thirds of the women of working age (1.8 million) were still in households; by 1984, the number remaining outside the paid labor force was only .26 million. The majority of women still in the household are over forty years of age, unskilled, and live in small agricultural villages where nonagricultural employment possibilities are limited.[6]

Data in Table 2 (Chapter 5) indicate that the Hungarian female labor force participation rates in 1984 were high, especially in relation to Austria (10 percentage points higher), where they were declining. However, this was not the case in relation to other socialist countries in Eastern Europe. Furthermore, the increase from 1975 to 1985 was the lowest of the four socialist countries for which data were given. In part, this may reflect the average age of the Hungarian population—22 percent of the population is now over retirement age—but it also may have something to do with Hungary's generous "special maternity allowances" (SMA). These were introduced in 1967, at a time when Hungarian manpower planners were anticipating the possibility of unemployment because of the forthcoming introduction of the New Economic Mechanism and the maturing of the generation born during the Ratko period.[7]

As of 1981, Hungarian mothers who use up their six months' full-salary maternity pay may remain at home until their child reaches the age of three, while their employment status and all social insurance rights remain uninterrupted. During the time of this special maternity leave (after 1985) they are to receive 75 percent of their former earnings (equivalent to sick pay) until the child reaches the age of eighteen months (as of 1986). This allowance provides for a minimum payment of 2,500 forints and a maximum of 4,500 forints per month, compared to an average wage of 5,800 forints.[8] After the child reaches the age of eighteen months and until the age of three, families receive a flat 1,340 forints per month as "child-care aid." This is in addition to the 710 forints per month "family allowance," so that total payments come to over 2,000 forints per month per child, including the child-care aid. The family allowance can continue until the offspring reaches twenty-four years of age, or as long as he or she is in school.

If we count women receiving home leave payments as "employed," then 82 percent of Hungarian women with children less than three years of age are participating in the labor force, compared to 80 percent in the GDR where the family allowances are shorter and less generous. Initially, in 1967, Hungarian feminists opposed this legislation, claiming that it discouraged the full participation of women in labor. However, judging by the fact that this institution has spread outside Hungary to such tight labor markets as those of the GDR and the USSR, as well as to Sweden and Denmark, it has apparently proven to be popular with young women, particularly those in routine jobs.[9]

One of the demands of Solidarity in Poland was that a similar paid maternity allowance program be instituted for Polish women.[10] This demand was accepted by the government and has produced the same result as in Hungary: a significant short-run bulge in the Polish birth rate (which was relatively high due to the influence of the Catholic church) between 1981 and 1983. Today Poland has the second highest birth rate in Europe, just below Moslem Albania.

Hungarian statistical handbooks present average wage data for *all* workers (men and women), as well as separate data for women. Nevertheless, it is possible to calculate men's and women's wages separately, as is conventionally done in the West. However, this is not possible for the German Democratic Republic or the USSR. Various other sources conclude that Hungarian women's wages are between 70 and 75 percent of men's wages with a slight tendency for the sex gap to close. Likewise, in agriculture, women's wages seem to approximate 70 percent of men's wages on average.[11]

Part of the gap can be explained by differences in the average education of men and women. In 1980, 71.1 percent of males fifteen and older had completed eight years of primary education; the percentage for females was only 61.6. If we look at secondary schools, we find that only 24.6 percent of the graduates of agricultural vocational secondary schools were women. Among graduates of industrial vocational secondary schools, 25.8 percent were women, while 99.8 percent of the graduates of kindergarten teaching schools (a field in which wages are extremely low) were women.

As in the USSR (but not in the United States), women are excluded from underground coal mining, the highest-paid occupation in both Hungary and the USSR. In Hungarian mining, (principally coal), average wages in 1984 were 8,096 forints per month—44 percent higher than the average wage generally. Clearly, part of the difference between average wages for men

Table 3

Women as a Percentage of University Students in Hungary, the German Democratic Republic, and the USSR, 1980s

Discipline	Percentage of female graduate students in Hungary, 1987	Percentage of female students in the GDR, 1982	Percentage of female students in the USSR, 1985-86
Technical science	19.1	26.5	44.0
Agricultural science	34.9	50.1	36.0
Economics	64.9	62.3	71.0
Medicine	52.4	55.2	60.0
Pharmacy	80.4	n.a.	n.a.
Other health	95.0	n.a.	n.a.
Veterinarian	19.1	n.a.	n.a.
Philosophy, history, and philology	64.7	35.0	n.a.
Law	57.2	n.a.	n.a.
Natural science	48.1	54.8	n.a.
Pedagogy	74.1	74.5	74.0
Teachers college	89.6	n.a.	n.a.
Kindergarten teaching	99.6	n.a	n.a.
Physical education	34.0	35.8	n.a.
Art	53.4	43.5	n.a.

Sources of data:
Hungary: *Statistical Pocketbook of Hungary, 1987,* p. 70.
German Democratic Republic: G. E. Edwards, *GDR Society and Social Institutions* (New York: St. Martin's Press, 1985).
USSR: *Vestnik Statistiki* 1 (1987), 58.

and women can be explained by the greater disutility of certain types of labor associated with jobs typically considered to be men's occupations.

If we look at higher education in Hungary today, the percentage of the eighteen to twenty-two year old cohorts attending tertiary schools was 9.9 in 1984, of whom 51.4 percent were women (compared to 52 percent in the USSR). Thus, given time, the average gap between men's and women's years of education should tend to close. The percentages of female graduates in Hungary in 1984 are compared with the percentages of women in tertiary education in the USSR and the GDR in the 1980s in Table 3. In general, the Soviet and East German percentages for women in various traditionally male occupations appear to be higher, and the Soviet and East German percentages for women in the feminized professions are lower.

One positive index of the status of women is a high divorce rate, particularly if the initiators of divorce proceedings are women. In 1982, there were 2.7 divorces per thousand in Hungary, compared with 3.0 in the GDR, 3.1 in Cuba, and 3.3 in the USSR.[12] Next door in Czechoslovakia the rate is only 2.2. Romania has a rate of 1.5, the same as in Bulgaria. In Catholic Poland, it is only 1.3. About two-thirds of all Hungarian divorces are initiated by women, although this may be a formality, according to Hungarian sociologists, since in some cases the real initiators are men, and women are merely instituting the proceedings. As mentioned above, the deduction of child support payments from fathers is much facilitated by the fact that the state is the employer in most cases.[13]

Another index of women's liberation is the abortion rate per 1,000 women between the ages of fifteen and forty-nine. In 1984, it was 3.3, up from 3.1 in 1980, but down from 7.2 in 1970, before there was a tightening of legalized abortion legislation. The percentage of Hungarian women (aged seventeen to forty-nine) taking contraceptive pills has risen from 6.7 in 1970 to 32.4 in 1984. In contrast to Hungary's liberalization of abortion and birth control, abortion has been illegal in neighboring Romania since 1967, and a four-child family is considered to be the ideal. In Bulgaria, abortion is restricted to women already having two children.[14]

The development of a thriving second economy in the past decade may have meant more income for many Hungarian families, but the share of housework done by women has probably risen since men are the predominant participants in the second economy. The reduction of the official Hungarian workweek to five days (forty to forty-two hours) has led to more second economy activity on the part of Hungarian men, beginning in the mid-eighties.

Hungarian sociologists have recently studied two generations of women—the current generation and their mothers, who were young during the Stalinist Rakosi years. Not surprisingly, they found that the earlier generation of young women felt that there had been many more opportunities for advancement for themselves than is the case with their daughters.

While there is no independent women's movement in Hungary—and Western-type feminism is virtually nonexistent—there have been some instances in which women have successfully pressured the government to change its policies. A recent minor victory for Hungarian women was the legislation allowing men to stay home and receive special maternity allowances. This is particularly helpful to families in which the woman's wage exceeds that of her spouse.

Discrimination Against Gypsies in Hungary

The greatest concentration of Gypsies in the world today can be found in Central and Southeastern Europe. Over one million are distributed fairly equally among the populations of Hungary, Czechoslovakia, Romania, and Bulgaria. Gypsies originated in India, but for many years certain tribes were confined under Czarist serfdom to Bessarabia, or what is now Moldavia. After the ending of serfdom in Russia in 1861, these tribes spread all over the world where they were characterized by their high levels of mobility.

Hitler, of course, devised a policy designed to provide a permanent solution to the "Gypsy problem." In the case of

Hungary, 80,000 Gypsies (out of 230,000) lost their lives in fascist extermination camps. About the same number of Polish Gypsies perished in the holocaust, according to Professor Leshevsky, and altogether as many as 70 to 80 percent of the European Gypsy population—a half million Gypsies—may have perished in the camps and during the war.[15] As a result, there are very few remnants of the prewar Gypsy communities in either Poland or the Germanies.[16]

Government policies and attitudes toward Gypsies vary greatly throughout the world. In most Western countries, Gypsies constitute a very minor group, and no special effort is made to integrate them. In the United States and France, they frequently travel in campers or mobile homes and are sometimes the subject of popular, romantic movies such as *Angelo, My Love* and *King of the Gypsies.*[17] Great Britain has established special campgrounds for Gypsies and for "tinkers," who are often confused with Gypsies, to allow them to retain their "romantic" way of life. In Eastern European countries, including the USSR, governments have attempted to reduce Gypsy nomadism and have tried to integrate them into the mainstream, sometimes with affirmative action levers such as heavily subsidized housing.[18]

Hungary is a good example of a socialist country trying to assimilate its one-half million Gypsies, who constitute about 5 percent of the total population.[19] Perhaps 60 percent of its Gypsy population has been assimilated, but 40 percent are living in what might charitably be called rural ghettos in about two thousand small towns. About one-third are living below the poverty line, and another one-third are living near the poverty line. These Gypsies are concentrated in certain areas, the most important of which lies east of Miskolc near the Soviet border. About 30 percent of all Hungarian Gypsies live in this area, and in some communities 10 to 60 percent of the population may be Gypsy. Many Gypsy men commute for several weeks at a time to Budapest or Miskolc, where better-paid work for unskilled labor is available.

An important institution being used to assimilate Gypsy males is the Hungarian armed forces. In 1979, a decree recognized the army's failure to attract enough Gypsies and urged that more positive steps be taken to increase the percentage of Gypsy males being drafted.[20] At present, about three-fourths of all Gypsy males in the draft age group are selected; the rest are rejected for medical reasons.

It is sometimes recognized that interwar Hungary had an "Indian problem" with respect to its Gypsies, but that today the country is facing a "black problem." The postwar regime has produced a small group of Gypsy intellectuals who are uninterested in assimilation and who are seeking to represent the Gypsies as an ethnic group. One of their demands, which was granted in 1987, was for a newspaper in their own language (Rom). Other ethnic minorities—Romanians, Germans, Slovaks, and Croatians—have their own newspapers.

There are a number of similarities between the perceptions and conditions of Hungarian Gypsies today and those of United States blacks thirty years ago. They are supposedly especially talented in music and the arts.[21] One of the ways in which Gypsies improved their relative status was by playing in most state-operated Budapest restaurants. While this was prevalent in the sixties, there has apparently been a decline in the importance of this avenue of escape from poverty, especially now that many restaurants have been contracted out to private individuals, who are more profit-oriented and thus less tolerant of covert unemployment.

Other Hungarians take a more paternalistic view of the Gypsies, emphasizing their childlike character, lack of industriousness, criminal tendencies, and irresponsibility. Lower literacy rates and higher school drop-out rates are still the rule for Gypsies. Fertility rates are indeed higher, and life expectancy is fifteen years lower than that of the non-Gypsy population.

There is an important difference between the role of Gypsy women in Hungary and that of black women in the United States. Whereas the black family in the United States is frequently a matriarchy with very high female labor force participation rates, the Gypsy family is still strongly patriarchal. The male labor force participation rate for Gypsies is about the same as that of other Hungarian males, but female labor force participation rates are considerably lower—50 percent as compared to 80 percent for the non-Gypsy women. Only about one-half of the Gypsy women have been able to enter the labor force; the remainder languish at home in rural communities where outside employment is difficult, if not impossible, to obtain. Special maternity allowances help only those who were in the paid labor force before they began having children. Since Gypsy women tend to marry at a very early age, usually before they have work experience, they are frequently ineligible for the SMAs. Gypsies are also shortchanged when it comes to pensions and family allowances.

Although there is a high labor force participation rate for Gypsy males, there are great differences between the skills of Gypsies and non-Gypsies. Fifty percent of Gypsies are unskilled as compared to only 12 percent of non-Gypsies. Eight percent of Gypsies are skilled and 30 percent of non-Gypsies are skilled—the balance of 27 percent of Gypsies and 43 percent of non-Gypsies are semi-skilled.

There are many more dependents per Gypsy worker—two and one-half times more than for non-Gypsies. The age structures of the two populations are very different. Thirty-eight percent of the Gypsy population is between zero and fourteen, while only 21 percent of the non-Gypsy population is this young.[22] Ten percent of Gypsies and 22 percent of non-Gypsies are above retirement age.

The main forms of affirmative action in Hungary today relate to housing allocation, free land, and low or zero interest rates. Hungary's non-Gypsies probably resent affirmative action programs, as do non-blacks in the United States. This resentment may intensify as average levels of living improve slowly in the eighties. Nevertheless, the government persists in its policies for a number of reasons, the most important of which is that there are growing numbers of Gypsy intellectuals who are proud of their ethnic background and are unwilling to "pass" as non-Gypsies. In addition, the existence of rural slums no doubt represents a blight on what Hungarians would like to show the outside world.[23]

Still, the Hungarians have not gone as far as the Czechs near Most (Bohemia) and Kosice (Slovakia), where housing authorities have constructed segregated high-rise apartments much like those in central cities in urban America. Czech Gypsy experts will defend the segregated high-rise apartment buildings as being necessary to maintain Gypsy support systems at this stage in their development.

Poverty is as much a relative condition as it is an absolute one. Now that luxury goods are appearing in Hungarian shops, the still abysmal condition of some Gypsies is even more unsettling. Prior to the beginning of the New Economic Mechanism in 1968, and particularly during the period of Stalinist rule under Rakosi, Hungarian women and Gypsies enjoyed a better standard of living, as compared with non-Gypsy males, than they do today.

While educated women and Gypsies have done quite well, the average gap between the general population and the victims of discrimination has probably widened in the past twenty years. As in the United States, there would appear to be a trade-off between full employment and affirmative action. To the extent that the New Economic Mechanism has permitted the development of a buyers' market for labor, more affirmative action, rather than less, would seem to be called for.

8

Conclusions

There is considerable agreement among leading economists, including Nobel Prize winners Sir Arthur Lewis, Gunnar Myrdal, and James Tobin, that the most effective destroyer of discrimination is rapid economic growth. The experience of the sixties, when the New Economics and the Vietnam War propelled the United States economy forward, bears this out for blacks.[1] By the same token, the comparatively sluggish condition of the economy after 1966 and especially after 1973 has not been conducive to improving the relative economic position of *average* nonwhites and females. Nevertheless, *marginal* (or most productive) nonwhites and women have done remarkably well, thanks to the implementation of affirmative action programs, reinforced by rising expectations of young women stimulated by the women's liberation movement.

Within the nonwhite and female communities, especially the white and nonwhite female-headed family, average conditions have deteriorated.[2] We can assume that the Gini coefficients, or indexes of income concentration, for both nonwhites and unmarried women have been rising, that is, the respective income distributions for these groups are becoming more unequal. Between 1974 and 1979, the Gini coefficient for blacks rose from .389 to .410.[3]

It can be argued that affirmative action programs are a substitute for genuine full employment. If we had managed to keep our economy operating closer to full employment, as we did during World War II, the Korean conflict, and the first part of the Vietnam War years, the sellers' market for labor power would have given nonwhites and women greater bargaining power. As a result, discrimination would have been less possible and affirmative action less imperative, just as it probably is today under "actually existing socialism."[4]

Just as there is a trade-off between full employment and the need for affirmative action, so too is there also some trade-off between the macroeconomics and the microeconomics of the discrimination problem in a FL economy. To the extent that firms practice affirmative action, and as a result have higher productivity, this releases resources that had formerly represented disguised, or covert, unemployment. When the disguised unemployment is brought out into the open, the macroeconomic problem appears to worsen. On the other hand, if discrimination and segregation both represent an inefficient use of resources, disguised unemployment rises at the microeconomic level and the macroeconomic problem of achieving full employment appears to be less compelling.[5]

New Left economists have argued that the practice of racism and sexism is useful to employers since it allows the capitalist to play one group against the other.[6] There is certainly some support for this view in past history, particularly in the use of blacks as strike-breakers. But the working class can be divided in many ways other than by race or sex. At the present time, it is divided principally between the employed and the unemployed. A new form of discrimination, however, has also developed in recent collective bargaining agreements. Negotiators for workers have been asked to accept two-tier settlements—lower pay and/or fringe benefits for "new workers" as opposed to the older experienced labor force. There has also been an attempt by the Reagan administration to play off teenagers against adults by setting lower minimum wages for the former. In addition, there is competition between prison labor and free labor, as well as "outwork" in "electronic cottages" versus work in factories and offices.[7]

A decision has apparently been made since 1979 to bite the proverbial Friedmanian or Hayekian bullet and restore the operations of the Phillips curve.[8] The extremely tight monetary policy followed by the Federal Reserve under the leadership of Paul Volcker has produced the highest *real* interest rates since the Great Depression and the longest such period of the twentieth century. But it has also broken the back of inflation, as predicted by the Phillips curve.

When unemployment reaches double-digit proportions, labor—both unionized and nonunionized—is more interested in job security than it is in wage increases. As a result, the annual wage increases in the eighties have been 3 percent or even less, compared to 6 percent or more after 1966 and the breakdown of the Kennedy-Johnson price-wage guidelines. In some instances, wage give-backs have been required to save jobs.

What residual supply-side inflation is left in the United States economy today comes from the capital side rather than from the labor side of the market. The poor productivity of capital (low capacity utilization rates and higher unit overhead costs), as well as the higher price of capital (*real* interest), insures that unit capital costs rise at the same time that unit labor costs fall. This is certainly true in years when labor productivity is rising, as in the expansion of 1983 and the first half of 1984.[9]

It might be argued that, superficially, the Reagan administration has brought down the rate of unemployment to the level inherited from President Carter. This is not really the case, since what is needed is a comparison of age-adjusted unemployment rates. In the early seventies, this was a very popular calculation by the Council of Economic Advisers since it *reduced* the crude, or unadjusted, unemployment rate by about one percentage point. In the eighties, it is just the reverse, as can be seen from data in Table 4, which contains age-adjusted unemployment rates using 1956 as a "normal year." After age-adjusting, the Reagan unemployment rates until 1987 have been higher than those under Carter. The rate was 6.4 percent

Table 4

Age-Adjusted Civilian Unemployment Rates, United States, 1968-87

Year	Crude unemployment rate	Age-adjusted unemployment rate	Difference between two rates
1968	3.6	3.2	0.4
1969	3.5	3.1	0.4
1970	4.9	4.5	0.4
1971	5.9	5.3	0.6
1972	5.6	4.9	0.7
1973	4.9	4.2	0.7
1974	5.6	4.8	0.8
1975	8.5	7.5	1.0
1976	7.7	6.8	0.9
1977	7.1	6.2	0.9
1978	6.1	5.2	0.9
1979	5.8	5.0	0.8
1980	7.1	6.4	0.7
1981	7.6	6.9	0.7
1982	9.7	9.0	0.7
1983	9.6	9.1	0.5
1984	7.5	7.1	0.4
1985	7.2	6.8	0.4
1986	7.0	6.7	0.3
1987	6.2	5.9	0.3

Source: Handbook of Labor Statistics, *Monthly Labor Review*, calculations by Professor Robert Horn, James Madison University, as published in *Challenge*, July-August, 1988, 57.

under President Carter in 1980, compared with 6.7 percent under President Reagan in 1986.[10]

The reason for this phenomenon is that President Carter was working with teenagers who were the last of the baby boomers, while President Reagan has been benefiting from the relatively few teenagers who are in the vanguard of the baby busters. Since teenagers have significantly higher unemployment rates in general, this gives a downward bias to the recorded, or unadjusted, Reagan unemployment rates. It should also be remembered that the last Carter year (1980) was a recession year, while the second half of 1984 and the years thereafter were only "growth recession" years.

The typical United States capitalist now has the best of all worlds in the era of secular stagnation (nee stagflation). There has been double-digit unemployment to keep wage increases at a minimum, and affirmative action to increase labor productivity, lower costs of production, and maintain profit margins. Now that outright racism and sexism are apparently impermissible —due in part to international political pressures—employers play off the employed against the unemployed and the older employees against the newly hired. The larger the body of unemployed, the smaller the wage increases because job security becomes a paramount consideration even for unionized workers.[11] The increase in real wages per employed worker in 1983 and 1984—the only significant increase since 1972—was obtained at the expense of the growing number of unemployed workers by those fortunate enough to still be employed.

If the above analysis is correct, doesn't it imply that the sit-ins, marches on Washington, even riots in the streets in the mid-sixties, were unnecessary or unimportant? Far from it. As mentioned earlier, the threat by A. Phillip Randolph to march on Washington brought about FDR's Executive Order #8802 in 1941. Likewise, it might also be argued that Martin Luther King, Jr.'s march on Washington in 1963 accelerated the Civil Rights Act of 1964. The administrations of government-backed projects such as the San Francisco subway system (BART) paid little attention to broad legislative hints that they should use affirmative action guidelines.[12] It took grassroots protest and the boycott of a major St. Louis construction project in 1966 to put some backbone into government demands. The doors to greater opportunity must be *pushed* open, even if resistance today is less than that in the period before 1948.

In a political democracy, there are some issues and policies that are apparently too important to be determined by majority rule. In other words, there are some issues that should never be put on election ballots or subject to referenda. A good example of this is any proposal (such as Proposition 13 in California or 2 1/2 in Massachusetts) that calls for a reduction in tax rates. Once these propositions were passed, public education was squeezed to an undue extent in both California and Massachusetts. Other instances in which it would appear inadvisable to permit majoritarian decision making include such issues as balanced budget amendments, capital punishment, abortion, foreign aid, and the space program.[13]

I would argue that anything racist or sexist should also be kept off the ballot. While the state power elite can be nonracist and even nonsexist in the interests of international political relations or world public opinion, the majority of the population is still capable of being racist and sexist.[14] According to public opinion polls, three-fourths of all Americans oppose "equal" employment opportunity programs that give special "preference" ("quotas," guidelines) to certain groups. If we can disregard the poor phrasing of the question in which the word "quota" is used inappropriately, we can assume that this is another case where the state overrides popular will in the interest of creating a society that is more presentable to the outside world.[15]

One of the goals of this study has been to compare the affirmative action programs of the two superpowers with similar programs in more or less comparable countries in the two economic systems. It is not difficult to find conclusive evidence supporting the proposition that Canada and Western Europe have lagged behind the United States in introducing and developing affirmative action programs.[16]

The comparison of affirmative action programs in Hungary and the USSR is a more complex matter, however. For one thing, we are dealing with countries that have had very different political histories in the era of the cold war. During the postwar years and until the political upheaval of 1956, there was a vigorous affirmative action program in Hungary directed at both women and Gypsies—one which was modeled after the postrevolutionary experiences of the USSR. In the years after 1956, the Kadar government has been highly successful in building broad political support for its overall program. To do so, however, it has been necessary for the government to come down on the side of majority opinion, even if traditional socialist ideology has been sacrificed or become a bit frayed.[17] Thus, the soft-pedaling of affirmative action programs—which are not accepted by the majority in Hungary any more than they are in the United States—has been one practical means of developing broader popular support for the Kadar government. The growth of buyers' market forces and the weakening of central planning, particularly since the development of the New Economic Mechanism (NEM) in 1968, has tended to benefit the stronger members of society—Hungarian non-Gypsy males—as Sowell and the Chicago NFL school would probably predict.[18]

The deliberate, planned deindustrialization of the Hungarian economy since the introduction of the NEM has produced relatively fewer jobs in heavy industry and manufacturing and has encouraged the development of private activities in the service sector. Thus, as consumers and principal homemakers rather than as producers, Hungarian women have benefited relative to Soviet women in recent years. For example, they receive more generous maternity allowances; have access to contraceptives, home and appliance repair services, and make-up shops that explain the use of cosmetics;[19] and they do not have to face long lines for shopping as do their Soviet counterparts. In most indexes of women's liberation, however, Soviet women still have some advantages over their Hungarian counterparts: higher female labor force participation rates, less crowding into traditionally "feminine" occupations, and higher divorce rates.

It is difficult to compare the treatment of Gypsies in Hungary with that in the USSR. For one thing, Gypsies make up 5 percent of the Hungarian population, whereas they constitute less than 1 percent in the Soviet Union.[20] There is also an unevenness in the treatment and living conditions of Gypsies in both countries. Areas that have more recently joined the USSR, such as Moldavia or the part of the Ukraine that was formerly Czech Ruthenia, still seem to have greater problems than the areas which have been under Soviet influence since the revolution. In Hungary, areas in the northeast have more serious problems due to a greater concentration of Gypsies. The smaller Gypsy population of Budapest, on the other hand, is more integrated and dispersed than the populations of some small towns where ghettoization is still evident.

Generalizations about Gypsies are dangerous, but there does seem to be considerable fondness, and even admiration, among Soviets for the Soviet Gypsy population. In contrast, there is a distinct feeling of distaste for Gypsy culture to be found among large segments of the Hungarian population. For example, many Hungarians confess to disliking Gypsy music, but will put up with it in restaurants primarily because that is what Western tourists expect to find there.[21]

While Hungarian authorities are somewhat stymied in their pursuit of affirmative action for Gypsies and, to some extent, for women, this is less of a problem for Soviet authorities. Soviet dissidents, including those who emigrate, tend to be more racist and sexist than the average citizens who usually support the official nonracist, nonsexist policy of the state. Thus, the call for the reintroduction of women's committees in factories and other organizations by Premier Gorbachev at the 27th Party Congress might be interpreted as a first response to exogenous forces which have influenced Soviet decision making with respect to women.[22] In his address to the Central Committee on January 27, 1987, Gorbachev declared: "In order to meet our country's needs today, we must actively involve women in running the economy and culture on an all-Union or republican scale."

In his presummit NBC interview with Mikhail Gorbachev, Tom Brokaw asked: "Do you think that women should be spending more time at home in the traditional role of mother and homemaker?" Gorbachev replied: "No, I think women should take part in all spheres of life, in all processes taking place in society. But this must be done in such a way that one should not prejudice the other, and, moreover, we should think about how to help our women combine active participation in social, cultural processes with their duties, with their predestination, that is, as keeper of the homefires, of the family guardian, or the family. A strong family means a strong society. So, we will not restrict the participation of women in public affairs. We will rather help women so that it is easier for a woman to combine the function of motherhood, the role of mother, and the role of an active citizen of the country."[23]

The USSR's affirmative action policies toward women and Gypsies seem to be superior to those of Hungary, although this difference is not as clear-cut as that between the United States and Canada.[24] If we can assume a continuation of the Kadar program, we should expect the differences between Hungary and the USSR to be magnified over time. On the other hand, socialist countries in Eastern Europe have been noted for their volatility in the past. Who can predict what will occur in the Grosz years?

My overall conclusions for the advanced capitalist system as regards the relative role of the state and the market in "actually existing capitalism" are clearly at odds with those of the Chicago school. Sowell et al. place their faith in the operations of the market to improve conditions for minorities; however, it is my belief that the advanced capitalist market is increasingly failing to provide the dynamism to create labor market conditions that would reduce discrimination. It is therefore imperative for the advanced capitalist state to intervene in furthering the relative welfare of minorities. This is especially the case for the advanced capitalist superpower. It is not affirmative action that has failed, as hypothesized by neoconservatives like Charles Murray or

Nathan Glazer. Rather affirmative action has to some extent disguised the growing failure of the market in the advanced capitalist system.[25]

Why Is the Advanced Capitalist Market Failing?

It is difficult, if not impossible, for most mainstream NFL economists to imagine that anything might have gone wrong with the operations of free markets. There are certainly many positive results to be obtained from the operation of market forces at the microeconomic level. The tentative movement of the Gorbachev and post-Mao regimes toward the release of previously constrained market forces at the microeconomic level represents a recognition of this important fact of life.

It is primarily at the macroeconomic level that the advanced capitalist system—as distinct from the capitalism of the nineteenth and early twentieth centuries—increasingly shows signs of employment-creating, nonprogressive laws of motion. The secular growth of slack in the advanced capitalist system over the past two decades, and especially after 1973, seems somehow related to a falling rate of return to capital in an era when capital is no longer the scarce factor of production relative to labor power. As the founding father of the Chicago school, Frank Knight, recognized in the early twenties, this change in factor proportions should theoretically require some diminution in the expected rates of return to capital as well as some increase in the relative share of total income in the form of wages and salaries.

There is little evidence that the relative share of total income going to wages and salaries has declined, as Karl Marx had predicted; nor is there any relative shift in favor of workers. Instead, there have been shifts within the returns to capital that are, in my view, counterproductive. Income payments in the form of interest have grown at the expense of income in the form of profits. In other words, there is a growing antithetical relationship between lenders and borrowers. The Keynesian counterrevolution, beginning in 1951, has produced a dramatic rise in the share of total income going to the comparatively unproductive financial capitalist lenders, as opposed to the more productive industrial capitalist borrowers.

In addition, the important insights associated with classical Keynesians found in the *General Theory* (in contrast to the Keynes of the *Economic Consequences of the Peace* or the *Treatise on Money*) are all but forgotten. Instead of developments that would produce a euthanasia of the rentier, we have seen a relative enrichment of the rentier during the past forty years in the developing windfall economy. Instead of assuming a general equilibrium at less than full employment without government intervention, we now act as if Say's Law were still working as it did in the nineteenth century, and as it still does today in the Second (noncapitalist) and Third Worlds. Instead of deploring saving and assuming the paradox of thrift, we fret over the decline in the rate of personal savings in the United States. Instead of assuming that monetary policy should be as neutral or passive as possible, we have permitted a gradual reduction in the real money supply relative to the real gross national product. This is the ultimate basis for the longest extended period of high real interest rates in the twentieth century during the Reagan administration.

To understand the growing failure of the market at the macroeconomic level, it is necessary to look back on the 1920s, when there was an unparalleled operation of free market forces and a minimum of government intervention. On the surface, everything seemed to be coming up roses. Irving Fisher, who was the Paul Samuelson of that day, went so far as to predict in 1929 that we had achieved permanent prosperity. Labor productivity in the 1920s grew at the most rapid pace in our entire economic history. At the same time, money wages increased only modestly due to the growing weakness of trade unions and the falling price of food caused by persistent agricultural overproduction after World War I. Under such circumstances, profits boomed, as Ricardo might well have predicted. All was well in the short run as long as these profits were reinvested or ploughed back into new capacity to produce more goods.

Because of disarmament measures, expenditures on the military were infinitesimal. As a result, an intimate relationship between consumption and investment still existed, as posited by the newly conceived acceleration principle. Weaknesses in consumption developed as wages and salaries grew slowly relative to profits, interest, dividends, and rent. The distribution of income became more unequal, and by the end of the decade there was a serious *disproportionality* between the greater capacity to produce goods and the effective demand required to utilize this capacity.[26]

In the thirties, this failure of the market at the macroeconomic level seemed obvious. As a result, government intervention increased in order to offset the serious capital strike and the decline in private spending. The most successful interventions in the capitalist market took place in Germany, Japan, and, to some extent, Italy. Even before the publication of the *General Theory*, all of these countries began practicing classical Keynesian policies with neutralized monetary sectors. The United States under FDR somehow muddled through the thirties without resorting to classical Keynesian policies and in fact increased the independence of the Federal Reserve Board in 1935. It wasn't until early 1942 that Roosevelt finally neutralized the Fed for the duration of the war—with the cooperation of its populist chairman, Marriner Eccles. Roosevelt then began to practice classical Keynesian economics, including Abba Lerner's principle of functional finance, since it was deemed more important to defeat Hitler than to cool off what was clearly an overheated economy.[27]

World War II gave world capitalism a new lease on life, to the extent that large quantities of capital in Japan, Germany, and Great Britain were obliterated by Allied and Axis bombers. In addition, there was a large-scale repatriation of Japanese and German workers to their homelands from Asia and Eastern Europe.[28] This newly created abundance of labor relative to capital in effect turned these formerly advanced economies back to their nineteenth century factor proportions. It therefore justified the expected high rates of return to capital in the eyes of United States multinational corporations in their investments abroad. Say's Law seemed to be working again in the economies of the defeated countries, and the banking authorities could safely be reinstalled in their prefascist positions of power. The postwar "economic miracles" of the fifties and the sixties in both Japan and West Germany now become more understandable.

The United States and Canada experienced a greater problem in the postwar years since no capital had been destroyed in either country during the war. This problem was solved by developing Keynesian employment-creating institutions that permitted some modification of the formerly intimate relationship between consumption and investment. Investment became much more independent of consumption (and the possibility of a disproportion between the two was greatly reduced), to the extent that the state was willing to subsidize both consumption and investment. The following devices were used: accelerated depreciation allowances, foreign investment tax advantages, expansion of the Export-Import Bank, the Marshall Plan, foreign aid, non-repayable foreign loans, Public Law 480 shipments, food stamps, and, most important, the growth of the military-industrial complex.

It is important to compare the operations of capitalism in Canada, which was less affected by the subsidies to consumption and investment. Until the devaluation of the Canadian dollar in 1961—ten years before Richard Nixon applied the same opportunistic beggar-thy-neighbor prescription for the United States economy—Canada had the worst overall growth record in the advanced capitalist system. It was only by deliberately turning the terms of trade against itself—or what George Gilder refers to as "exchange rate mercantilism"—that Canada was able to price its products back into world markets, including the grain markets of the noncapitalist countries.

While the Allied Control authorities restored the prewar role of bankers in Japan and West Germany during the late forties, the Fed did not become independent in the United States until March 1951, in the midst of the Korean War. Thereafter, secular inflation disguised the negative, or insignificant, real interest rates until the Reagan era. But the basis for the high plateau of real interest rates in the 1980s was being slowly constructed after 1951. As a consequence of the Federal Reserve's bias toward expected inflation and its chronic policy to cool off an economy that was increasingly underheated after 1966, we have painted ourselves into an extremely awkward corner.

This underheated economy still showed increasing amounts of inflation, but not because of too much demand in the system. On the contrary, after 1966, inflation came, more often than not, from the supply side of the market rather than the traditional demand side. This resulted principally from rising overhead costs per unit, the OPEC cartel, sales taxes at the state and local level, excise taxes, sluggish labor productivity in the growing and crowded service sector, environmental protection, and, eventually, in the eighties, from the high real interest rates themselves. Ultimately, the back of supply-side inflation was broken by the Fed under Paul Volcker as a result of double-digit unemployment during the sharp recession of 1981 to 1982 and subsequent workers' preferences for job security over money wage increases.

In the course of the past forty years, there have been two obvious attempts to revert to nineteenth century supply-side economics. The first occurred during the administrations of John F. Kennedy and Lyndon B. Johnson, and the second during the Reagan era. The short-run success of the investment tax credit of 1962 and the 1964 tax cut was followed by the growth of excess capacity after 1966. As a result, the Vietnam War was fought with increasing underutilization of capital and squeezed profits. In substance, under the "new economics" of Walter Heller and the Council of Economic Advisers, the United States now *planned* a disproportion between consumption and investment very similar to that produced by the free market in the 1920s.

The principal difference between the situation at the end of the 1920s and the economy after 1966 was that the welfare/warfare state had grown through state expenditures for the Vietnam War and the subsequent military buildup under Presidents Carter and Reagan. This built-in stabilizer effect—on the downside of what had been the business cycle—of the military-industrial complex (MIC) has made it so difficult for the United States to experience anything resembling the Great Depression, even after "Bloody Monday" on October 19, 1987. The higher rate of profit in MIC activities also moderates somewhat the decline in the overall rates of profit in the market sector.[29] The relative lack of increased military spending in Japan, Canada, and Western Europe, on the other hand, helps explain why the economic records for those countries in the 1980s have been inferior to that of the United States. It also explains why they are more vulnerable to external shocks.

Both Japan and West Germany have to some extent substituted huge export surpluses for domestic military spending. Nevertheless, their domestic economies have been extremely stagnant. As a result, their labor markets are weak, and female labor force participation rates have stagnated or decreased. West Germany has especially used an export surplus to the German Democratic Republic—financed by an interest-free "swing credit"—and to the Eastbloc in general. Japan relies more on export surpluses to noncapitalist China, and more recently to Vietnam, for similar reasons. Increasing trade with noncapitalist NFL economies which typically have little or no neomercantilist trade bias is a stabilizing factor in the advanced capitalist system. At the same time, these exports provide access to a higher level of technology and more overall utility for socialist countries. The United States rather chronically exports six or seven times as much as it imports from the USSR. Soviet gold—directly or indirectly—therefore becomes a necessary sterile import since it requires storage and guarding at Fort Knox or Zurich.

The relatively high real interest rates in the United States have produced a tendency for a strong dollar in the 1980s as foreigners prefer to park their "hot money" or liquid assets here in the form of interest-bearing Treasury bills. Secretary of the Treasury James Baker has succeeded in forcing Japan and West Germany to take part in a "dirty float," bringing about some weakening of the dollar relative to the Yen and the D-Mark. But the world value of the dollar remains remarkably high. This allows the United States to act as a mature creditor, accepting a chronic import surplus from the rest of the advanced capitalist system, just as Great Britain did in earlier times.[30]

At the microeconomic level, advanced capitalist pricing tends to be above a competitive equilibrium. Thus, relative surplus and surplus disposal are the basic economic problems of competitive units. To minimize this surplus, the European Economic Community regularly subsidizes exports through the value added tax, and other neomercantilist stimuli permeate the advanced capitalist system. In the United States, it is the Export-Import Bank which subsidizes exports and the International Trade Commission which discourages imports. This is done under the guise of preventing "dumping," yet it affects even the noncapitalist countries which have no real interest in dumping since they have chronic shortages due to their overall pricing below equilibrium. In the meantime, the burgeoning agricultural surpluses in the United States (which occur even after drought and after paying farmers not to cultivate acreage) are disposed of abroad under Public Law 480 and internally via the food stamp program.

It should be realized that these surpluses exist only under the assumption that nothing can be done to obtain a more egalitarian distribution of income. If our income could be redistributed away from savers in the direction of consumers, the oversupplies and general underutilization of our potential would be greatly reduced.

The growth of the role of state expenditures can overcome some of the weaknesses of the market despite the development of chronic buyers' markets for just about everything, including petroleum in the 1980s. This creeping realization problem— sometimes referred to by David Gordon as the "leaky balloon" hypothesis—has produced secular tendencies in place of formerly cyclical phenomena. It has even changed the nature and regularity of old-fashioned business cycles, as Schumpeter probably would have predicted in his criticism of Keynesian economics. While admitting the possibility of stabilizing the system, Schumpeter deplored the demise of the volatility represented by the business cycle. The double-dip recession of 1980 to 1982 and the long growth recession after the middle of 1984 are clearly unprecedented advanced capitalist developments which reflect the political business cycle and the growing role of the state in affecting the regularity and timing of fluctuations.

The Keynesian revolution and the developing realization problem produced by the Keynesian counterrevolution should also tend to shake one's faith in the contemporary relevance of Kondratiefs, or long waves of alternating twenty-five year periods of exhilaration and stagnation. A number of economists, including David Gordon of the New Left, have interpreted the sluggish overall growth of the past two decades as a reflection of an economy operating on the twenty-five year downside of a Kondratief. Walt Rostow, on the other hand, interpreted the inflation in raw material prices in the early 1970s as a reflection of operations on the upside of a Kondratief.[31] Clearly the phenomenon of rising prices from the supply side during a period of relative stagnation confounded both mainstream and non-mainstream economists.

Postwar changes in the operations of the advanced capitalist system would also seem to affect changes in fertility rates. Richard Easterlin has argued that we should expect twenty-year cycles in fertility rates: baby booms alternating with baby busts.[32] Thus far, this expectation has been unfulfilled. Fertility rates, after two decades of baby bust, remain well below rates necessary for replacement. Here again, continuity would seem to be a sounder expectation for our predictors than would periodic change.

At this late date, can anything be done to rectify our overall economic policy? The answer is yes, but it will require the adoption of policy that is completely at odds with supply-side economics, for supply-side economics produces good results in the short run and more excess capacity in the long run. There was a precedent for this about-face during the Ford administration when the president admitted such a dramatic shift in signing the House-initiated tax cut in March 1975. Six months earlier at the Economic Summit in September 1974, President Ford and Alan Greenspan, his new Chairman of the Council of Economic Advisers, had been plugging for a tax increase to "whip inflation now," even though the economy was already over ten months into the Great Recession of 1974-75.

What would an alternative economic policy based on classical Keynesian principles look like? It would first and foremost operate on the assumption that without government intervention there is a tendency toward equilibrium at less than full employment. Government spending is thus to be treated not as something to be avoided, but rather as an alternative to the failure of the market at the macroeconomic level. Both increases in government spending and reductions in tax rates are therefore required to mobilize resources that otherwise would be underutilized.[33] Although the Reagan administration's rhetoric calls for reductions in government spending and the cutting of tax rates, in practice it has increased federal spending at the same time that it has cut tax rates. This increase in federal spending as a percentage of gross national product is primarily, but not exclusively, related to the rapid growth of Pentagon spending and growth of interest on the debt. Thus, while we can appreciate the thrust of Reagan's fiscal policy, we may legitimately question the structure of the expenditure increases.

Under a FL economy, the rules for balancing the budget or minimizing the deficit are exactly the reverse of those required in a NFL framework. In the latter, operations at full employment can legitimately call for reductions in government spending and the raising of tax rates to reduce the active or structural federal deficit, as recommended by President Jimmy Carter and presidential aspirant Walter Mondale.

Unfortunately, these Democratic and Conservative Republican prescriptions (such as those of Senator Robert Dole) are inappropriate for an economy which operates chronically well within its potential, or production possibilities curve. This can be seen from the following historical postwar precedents. The sharp increase in military spending during the first year of the Korean conflict actually produced a significant surplus in the federal budget because previously unemployed resources which arose during the Truman recession of 1949 to 1950 began to pay taxes as the economy moved back to genuine full employment. Likewise, the cutting of tax rates in 1964 reduced the passive budget deficit and very nearly produced a balanced budget in 1965 for similar reasons.

The lesson that should have been learned from our postwar FL history is that *either* increases in government spending *or* the cutting of tax rates will improve the budget balance in an economy operating at less than full employment. Paradoxically, the common sense policy of cutting spending and raising tax rates to "balance the budget" will only reduce growth and worsen the passive budget deficit. This principle was temporarily recognized as valid by the Reagan supply-siders, such as Murray Weidenbaum, Reagan's first chairman of the Council of Economic Advisers, as increases in federal spending and sharp income tax reductions rescued the economy from the 1981-1982 recession. Weidenbaum commented at the time that his antirecession program was already in place when the Reagan recession struck. A natural question still arises: why was the post-recession economy still running huge passive federal deficits in 1983-1984, contrary to the earlier experiences of 1950-1951 and 1964-1965?

The answer can be found by comparing monetary policy in the two earlier periods with that of the Reagan era. In 1950-

1951, the Federal Reserve System was still neutralized until the Treasury Accord of March 1951. As a result, real interest rates were generally negative in the postwar years and continued to be minimal—at less than 2 percent—until the Reagan era. In the Kennedy years, the Fed, under William McChesney Martin, accommodated an easy fiscal policy until December 1965. In other words, there was minimal "leaning against the wind" on the part of the Fed, and this permitted improvements in the budget balance associated with the easy fiscal policies of the earlier years.

In contrast, the easier fiscal policy of Ronald Reagan has been partially vitiated by the very tight monetary policy followed by Paul Volcker, a Carter appointee who became chairman of the Fed in the fall of 1979. The Fed's violent "leaning against the wind" under Volcker has produced higher real interest rates in the 1980s. As noted in the *Economic Report of the President*, 1987, the real long-term interest rate from 1982 to 1986 has averaged 6.13 percent—about double the average rate over the past 130 years. This is clearly the longest continuous period of high real interest rates in the twentieth century.

These interest rates result in growing slack and large passive deficits which emanate from the failure of unemployed resources to contribute to federal revenues. Paradoxically, lower, or even nonexistent, real interest rates would mobilize tax-paying resources and eventually produce much smaller active or structural federal budget deficits. Considering the fact that interest charges for servicing the debt now account for approximately $100 billion annually and state and local budget surpluses—even in an economy operating on two cylinders—are running at $60 billion per year, an economy operating at genuine full employment would have a very small consolidated active or structural budget deficit.[34]

Our abnormally high real interest rates—which have generally exceeded those of other G-7 countries in the first half of the 1980s—also contribute to the persistent strength of the dollar in world money markets. This is true despite the Treasury's attempts to weaken the dollar in a dirty float among the leading G-5 countries following the Plaza Hotel agreement in the fall of 1985. Nevertheless, in 1987 the dollar was still much stronger in relationship to all countries with which we trade than it was at the beginning of the Reagan era.[35] It is the parking of foreign assets in this country—where they earn higher real interest—that accounts for the persistently strong dollar and the resulting foreign trade deficit.

Although it is fashionable to account for the foreign trade deficit by complaining about our "lack of competitiveness," there is little statistical evidence to support this assumption. The *Economic Report of the President*, 1987, concludes that the "deterioration of international cost competitiveness in United States manufacturing during the first half of the decade was the result of the real appreciation of the dollar, *not sagging productivity growth* [my emphasis] or excessive wage increases." Since 1981, manufacturing output per hour has grown at an average annual rate of 3.8 percent—46 percent faster than the postwar average of 2.6 percent per year. As a result, according to the Council of Economic Advisers, the growth in unit labor costs during the first half of the 1980s was 5 percent higher abroad than it was in the United States.

Thus far, only one major presidential aspirant of either party has recognized the ultimately pernicious consequences of Paul Volcker's slaying of the inflation dragon. Representative Jack Kemp's criticism of the Fed at the 1984 Republican Convention stands out as a brave recognition of an important truth. These high real interest rates, while curbing inflation, have another darker side. They contribute to the increased inequality in the distribution of income, the increase in numbers of people living below the poverty line (including the homeless and "couch people," who move in with friends or relatives), the domestic high passive federal deficit, the foreign trade deficit, and the decline in the velocity of money since 1981.

If the above analysis of the present dilemma has any validity, what is to be done? What is required is a chronic application of a triad of policies consisting of: (1) increased government spending, preferably of a nondefense nature; (2) cutting of tax rates, preferably with a "progressive" twist; and (3) neutralization of the Fed and very little concern over the twin deficits. Since the Reagan administration has in effect practiced these first two policies, the toughest nut to crack will be the third—reversing the trend of our monetary policy since 1951. This is particularly true since Paul Volcker's policy of slaying the inflation dragon is so popular with voters in the United States.

Even if we could somehow manage to put the Federal Reserve back into mothballs as we did from 1942 to 1951, there is still the problem of recognizing the necessity for a more egalitarian distribution of income. In this respect, we must recognize, at a minimum, the inappropriateness of consumption (or value-added) taxes, the folly of financing social security out of regressive taxation rather than progressive general revenues, the erosion of the once progressive income tax, and the dangers of encouraging inheritance as an institution. In short, we must abandon the nineteenth-century thinking of our grandparents in favor of an economics more appropriate for our grandchildren in the twenty-first century.

Notes

Introduction

1. Thomas Sowell, *Markets and Minorities* (New York: Basic Books, 1981), 106, 123. According to Sowell, "the volatility of government policy (with respect to minorities) suggests that determining its purpose over some meaningful span of time is also no easy task."

2. See Samuel Bowles and Richard Edwards, *Understanding Capitalism* (New York: Harper and Row, 1985), 194–95.

3. In the words of Michael Ellman, "full employment is a major achievement of state socialism. It is combined, however, with major problems of labor inflexibility, work morale, and lack of effort and interest by workers." See Michael Ellman, *Collectivization, Convergence and Capitalism: Political Economy in a Divided World* (London, Academic Press, 1984), 190. Also, Branko Horvat, *The Political Economy of Socialism* (Armonk, NY: M. E. Sharpe, 1982), 191 et seq. Horvat assumes that there is a third standard of reference, his version of participatory socialism. Thus, like the New Left in the United States, he concludes that both systems—capitalism and "etatism"—are "microeconomically as well as macroeconomically inefficient." Inflation is minimized in certain Soviet-type economies as a consequence of an "incomes policy" whereby money wage increases are less than increases in labor productivity.

4. An early version of these chapters appeared in *Development and Peace*, Autumn 1986, 81–94, published by the Institute of World Economy in Budapest.

Chapter 1

1. In the early days of Soviet planning—the so-called "extensive" stage of development—the USSR had a tremendous reserve of disguised unemployment, particularly in the agricultural sector, and could be less concerned with the law of value. Sustained interest in the efficiency of relative prices and in the elimination of subsidies as a general policy didn't take place until after 1949. This may be viewed as the watershed between an earlier employment-creating approach and the current employment-saving emphasis.

2. According to earlier versions of *Beyond the Wasteland*, the original title of the book was *Free Lunch*. While both *Monopoly Capital* and *Beyond the Wasteland* emphasize the surplus or waste, Baran and Sweezy look at it primarily as a demand problem, while Bowles et al. focus on the supply side. The present book regards it as a problem of *proportionality* between investment and consumption.

3. Say's Law goes back to a controversy between J. B. Say and Malthus over whether there could be a general overproduction problem, or glut. According to Say (and later conceded by Malthus), the income paid out in the production and investment process guaranteed that there was no real problem of this nature. Say's Law was sacrosanct until the publication of Keynes's *General Theory*.

4. See, for example, "Toward a More Competitive America," a five-part series sponsored by the Mobil Corporation in 1987, which appeared in *The New York Times*, *Time* magazine, and other leading publications. This is also one of Lester Thurow's prescriptions.

5. Alvin Hansen, who had originally been lukewarm in his reaction to the *General Theory*, was no doubt influenced by this event and became the leading United States Keynesian exponent of the secular stagnation hypothesis.

6. In all three cases, monetary policy was neutralized and fiscal policy predominated. In the case of Hitler, this was easier since his earliest writings were populist with respect to "parasitic" interest payments. For Japan, the neutralization of monetary policy required the assassination of the aged finance minister in 1936.

7. The multiplier was an early contribution of Richard Kahn to the Keynesian revolution. It is defined as the reciprocal of the marginal propensity to save. It emphasized the long-term indirect effects of government spending on total income which occurred as

a result of subsequent respending of the initial injection of purchasing power.

8. This principle of a difference between the "rate" and the "aggregate" is characteristic of a FL economy. It is a particularly important principle when applied to tax rates, because a lowering of tax rates may increase aggregate tax revenue, as was the case after the 1964 tax cut. But it is also applicable to profit rates and aggregate profits.

9. Since private investment is positively correlated with recent federal deficits, we must assume that "crowding in" is more realistic than "crowding out" as a description of our condition. See Robert Eisner, *How Real Is the Federal Deficit?* (New York: The Free Press, 1986), 178.

10. In the United States, real interest rates were very high in the early thirties as prices fell dramatically; money interest rates were sticky—a similarity between this period and the Reagan years. Nevertheless, the Reagan era represents the longest period of continuous high real interest in the twentieth century. According to the *Economic Report of the President*, 1987, the real long-term interest rate from 1982–86 has averaged 6.13 percent, or about double the average rate over the past 130 years. The real rate of interest continued rising in 1987.

11. See Arthur Ross, "The Negro in the American Economy," in: Arthur M. Ross and Herbert Hill, *Employment, Race and Poverty* (New York: Harcourt, Brace, and World, 1967), 3–48.

12. In this connection, see Lois Scharf, *To Work and to Wed: Female Employment, Feminism and the Great Depression* (Westport, CT: Greenwood Press, 1980), especially Chapter 3, "Governments, Working Wives, and Feminists."

13. In the course of a year, the Fed, which had been liberated from any influence by the Treasury in 1935, doubled the reserve requirements, supposedly because of inflationary expectations.

14. In the forties, when demand-pull inflation predominated, the consumer price index rose by about 70 percent compared with a 110 percent increase in the decade of the seventies, when supply-side inflation was primarily the rule. The annual rate of inflation in the 1940s was 5.6 percent compared with 7.8 percent in the 1970s. See Victor Perlo, *Super Profits and Crises: Modern U.S. Capitalism* (New York: International Publishers, 1988), 430.

15. Per capita consumption in the United States increased by 4 per-

cent in the thirties, 30 percent in the forties, and 15 percent in the fifties. See my *The Contrasting Economies* (Boston: Allyn and Bacon, 1963), 101.

16. For details of their criticism, see Leo Gruliow, *Public Soviet Views in the Postwar World Economy: An Official Critique of Eugene Varga's "Changes in the Economy of Capitalism Resulting from the Second World War"* (Washington, D.C.: Public Affairs Press), 1948.

17. The Fed was finally liberated by the Treasury Accord of March 1951, after which policy has been dictated by the fear of inflation. Since then we have seen a preference for "tight" monetary policy on the part of the monetary authorities.

18. In this connection, see John H. Hotson, "Ending the Debt-Money System," *Challenge*, March-April 1985, 48–50. According to Leonard Silk, "The Real Rate of Interest," *The New York Times*, 28 November 1984, D-2, during the sixties, the real rate of interest averaged 1.8 percent, and during the seventies it fell to 0.3 percent. See also Martin Feldstein, "Halving the Pain of Budget Balance," *Wall Street Journal*, 25 May 1988, 24.

19. See my "The Political Economy of Reparations," *New German Critique* (Winter 1973). This problem was recognized as early as March 1921 by John Foster Dulles in a speech at the Hyatt (nee Commodore) Hotel in New York City. The same dilemma faces the advanced capitalist system today as a result of the huge Third World debt. See also Alexander Cockburn, *Corruptions of Empire* (New York: Verso, 1987), 321–24.

20. Japan's failure to pay reparations to China was to some extent the result of the Maoist policy of "balanced equivalents," that is, trade between countries should be balanced with a minimum of international borrowing. Mao recalled the Boxer Rebellion, after which Imperial China was obliged to pay reparations to the Western Powers, resulting in considerable hardship for the Chinese people. As a result, he wished no similar hardship to be imposed on Japan. Now that the post-Mao government has opened itself up to foreign investment, and thereby rejected "balanced equivalents," Japanese reparations to China would still seem to be highly functional for both economies.

21. Public Law 480 was also referred to as "Food for Peace" in the Kennedy administration. It involves the exchange of United States agricultural surpluses for inconvertible local currencies, such as rupees, in the case of India. When now-Senator Daniel Patrick

Moynihan was Ambassador to India, he recognized the uselessness of these rupees and, in effect, had them burned. As a result of the Green Revolution, India is now more or less self-sufficient with respect to grain and no longer needs our surpluses. The Canadian government's construction of nuclear power plants in underdeveloped countries, including Romania, is equivalent to foreign aid and is basically un-profitable at the macroeconomic level, despite its employment-creating potential for Canada. It is profitable at the microeconomic level for the firms involved.

22. Leon Keyserling, who claimed to be a pragmatist but was ac-tually the last practicing Keynesian, played a major role in the draft-ing of National Security Council Report #68 in April 1950. This report outlined the usefulness of military Keynesianism in conducting the Cold War. In this connection, see Alan Wolfe, *America's Impasse: The Rise and Fall of the Politics of Growth* (Boston: South End Press, 1981). See also Bruce Steinberg, "The Military Boost in Industry," *Fortune*, 30 April 1984, 42–46, 48. Steinberg illogically assumes that military "industrial policy" is not particularly "efficient" since the same investment in the civilian economy could produce 25 percent more jobs. Thus, he infers efficiency to be a product of employment-creating rather than employment-saving.

23. Robert W. De Grasse, Jr., *Military Expansion, Economic Decline* (Armonk, NY: M. E. Sharpe, 1983), 47. This approach minimizes the "spin-offs" from military research and development for the private sector.

24. President Reagan's Economic Policy Advisory Board eventually recognized Heller's position by inviting him to join an outside group of twelve economists to advise the president on trade policy and pro-tectionism. See Martin Anderson, *Revolution* (New York: Harcourt Brace Jovanovich, 1988), 269.

25. There was a brief period in the late forties when Walter Reuther of the United Automobile Workers could welcome employment-saving automation, but this position was short-lived. It should be noted that Freeman and Medoff come to the conclusion that unionization is associated with greater productivity of labor. This may simply reflect the decision by management to substitute capital for more high-priced unionized labor and have little to do with the effort or interest of union workers.

26. Western European countries, however, have made certain progress in reducing the average workweek. In the Federal Republic

of Germany, a six-week strike by 400,000 workers at I. G. Metall in 1984 won a 37-hour workweek, to be phased in over a four-year period. Later, workers in Norway, Denmark, and Finland won 37 to 37.5-hour workweeks. Workers in the Netherlands have a 38-hour workweek. See *People's Daily World*, 17 July 1987, A-2.

27. Unemployment compensation has recently covered only about one-third of the total number of people unemployed. Prices in this second economy are weaker than they are in the aboveground economy, because both producers and consumers benefit from the avoidance of taxes. This represents another reason for the over-estimation of inflation by the official Consumer Price Index in the United States. And it represents an important underlying reason for large passive deficits.

28. DISCs permitted exporting firms to cooperate in pushing for larger export markets for the industry as a whole.

29. This opposition to the Fed showed up in the Republican platform in the 1984 election. This contrasts with the lack of criticism among the Democrats that year, to the possible exclusion of Jesse Jackson.

30. At the same time that taxes were cut, the Treasury conducted a stepped-up campaign designed to sell more bonds to the public.

31. After four months without an investment tax credit, President Johnson sheepishly announced the restoration of the ITC in the fall of 1966. This remained in effect until the Nixon administration, when it was again abandoned, only to be restored in connection with Nixon's New Economic Policy in the fall of 1971. From the second quarter of 1966 through the second quarter of 1967, real growth averaged only 2.4 percent, despite the surging expenditures in Vietnam. See Leonard Silk, "The Growth Recession," *The New York Times*, 14 June 1985, D-2.

32. See, for example, Eliot Janeway, *The Economics of Crisis, War, Politics and the Dollar* (New York: Weybright and Talley, 1968). This period represents a watershed between the time when Wall Street was bullish during the Vietnam War and when it became bearish.

33. In Canada, interest as a percent of gross national product rose from 2.1 to 8.2 percent between 1950 and 1987. Since World War II, net interest income increased 224-fold in Canada compared to 186-fold in the United States. See *C.O.M.E.R. Comments*, Volume 1, No. 1, Summer 1988, 1–2.

34. See Albert T. Sommers, *The U.S. Economy Demystified* (Lex-

ington, MA: Lexington Books, 1985), 117. According to Sommers, if M-1 were adjusted for inflation, its real volume would appear to be lower than it was fifteen years ago. The implications of the decline in the velocity of money after 1981 are the same as they were in the Great Depression—the impossibility of "pushing on a string."

35. A minor, once-only move toward employment-saving consisted of the elimination of the draft and the introduction of a volunteer armed services by President Nixon in 1973. Democrats have typically endorsed the draft, compulsory universal service, or registration for the draft (Carter), while Republicans have traditionally preferred employment-saving market forces. See my "Compulsory Military Service is Bad Economics," *The Hofstra Review* (Spring 1968), 1–4. The Soviet Union also pursues a counterproductive policy with respect to the draft since compulsory service represents a FL institution within a basically NFL economy. The same is also true for the Eastern European socialist countries. It should be pointed out that the draft is a socializing institution for minority groups. This might be used to rationalize the draft in countries with minority problems, such as Hungary with its Gypsy problem. Some would argue that Soviet authorities are faced with a similar problem in their drafting of minorities. See Martin Binkin and Mark Eitelberg, *Blacks and the Military* (Washington, D.C.: The Brookings Institution, 1982), 116–17

Chapter 2

1. A broader definition would have to include the factors responsible for the average productivity differentials among minorities, including women, in relationship to white male workers. Discrimination in childrearing and in education no doubt still accounts for differentials in average productivity within groups that are victims of discrimination.

2. See, for example, Citizens' Commission on Civil Rights, *Affirmative Action to Open the Doors of Job Opportunity: A Policy of Fairness and Compassion That Has Worked* (Washington, D.C., 1984). Also, Anne B. Fisher, "Businessmen Like to Hire by the Numbers," *Fortune*, 16 September 1985, 54 et seq. According to Fisher, "persuasive evidence indicates that most large corporations want to retain their affirmative action programs, numerical goals and all." Also, Alan Farnham, "Holding Firm on Affirmative Action," *Fortune*, 13 March 1989, 87–88. The initial reaction of big business to af-

firmative action was negative because this represented an increased government role in the business sphere. The reaction of the American Medical Association to Medicare and Medicaid was also negative at first, but the increased relative income for doctors since 1966 has changed their thinking on this score. Thus, both doctors and businessmen can indulge in a bit of "altruism" while they feather their own nests.

3. This position also seemed to be held by W. Arthur Lewis, who writes that "in general, pressure for discrimination comes not from employers but from other employees." Furthermore, "the interests of employers and white trade unions diverge. The employer wants to hire more blacks and fewer whites, and the unions want to protect the job by fixing its minimum wage at the level of the white." See his *Racial Conflict and Economic Development* (Cambridge: Harvard University Press, 1985), 38, 40. Richard B. Freeman and James L. Medoff, *What Do Unions Do?* (New York: Basic Books, 1984), found that black males are now about as unionized as white males were in 1977, despite the fact that they are considerably more anxious to join unions than are white males. By 1988, blacks accounted for 20% of union members in manufacturing and 50% of newly organized workers. See *The New York Times*, 18 January 1989, E-4. This increase in the unionization of black males has been a by-product of the Civil Rights Act of 1964, which was also directed at discriminating unions. Women are also more interested in joining unions than men, according to Cathy Trost, "More Family Issues Surface at Bargaining Talks as Women Show Increasing Interest in Unions," *Wall Street Journal*, 2 December 1986, 70. For an account of union opposition to affirmative action, see Herbert Hill, "Race, Ethnicity, and Organized Labor: The Opposition to Affirmative Action," *New Politics* (Winter 1987), especially 64–68.

4. The most obvious example of the dire effects of desegregation on black capitalists shows up in the rapid demise of the black baseball league after the integration of what had been lily-white baseball from 1890 to 1947. (There had been some integration in baseball up to 1890.) The virtual disappearance of films produced by blacks, which were common before World War II, is another example. Racist movies had no place in the wartime years, and Hollywood's optimistic integrationism, particularly in training films during the war, was more advanced than what was being practiced in the armed services. See Thomas Cripps, *Black Film as Genre* (Bloomington: Indiana Univer-

sity Press, 1979). Black teachers in the South resisted school desegregation after 1954. Even the recent plight of the nonprofit black colleges, such as Fisk University, was also to be expected as a result of affirmative action programs at predominantly white universities. Before the seventies, black institutions educated more than half of all black college students. In the eighties, they enrolled about 25 percent of all black students. See Margaret B. Wilkerson, "A Report on the Educational Status of Black Women During the UN Decade of Women, 1976–85," *The Review of Black Political Economy* (Fall-Winter 1985–86), 87.

5. Gary Becker, *The Economics of Discrimination* (Chicago: University of Chicago Press, 1957).

6. For a recent attempt to show how discrimination against women reduces GNP, see *Economic Report of the President*, 1987, 223. In my view, only potential GNP is reduced by discrimination.

7. To his credit, Herbert Hoover resisted the advice that he pursue a lower wage policy, pointing out that wages were an important source of purchasing power which we sadly needed.

8. It is interesting to note that "busing," which is used to integrate schools, also wastes capital. But the root of this problem lies in the pattern of residential housing brought about by de facto restrictive covenants, "redlining" by banks, and the federal government through the FHA. The level of housing segregation increased between 1960 and 1970 and declined slightly thereafter. See Ann B. Schnare, "Chicago's Dubious Achievement," *Illinois Business Review* (February 1987), 8–9.

9. In South Africa, white workers, encouraged by union and communist leaders, engaged in an armed rebellion against the government in order to prevent the employment of black Africans in the mines under conditions similar to theirs. This 1921 uprising (the Rand riots) marked the beginning of apartheid. For this and other evidence of racism among white South African workers, see Branko Horvat, *The Political Economy of Socialism* (Armonk, NY: M. E. Sharpe, 1982), 66.

10. Sir Roy Harrod, in his testimony before the Royal Commission on Equal Pay (1946), argued that "the situation [of unequal pay] has proved tolerable and stable because it has been found . . . to secure that motherhood as a vocation is not too unattractive compared with work in the professions, industry, or trade." See Elizabeth Wilson, "Thatcherism and Women: After Seven Years," in: Ralph Miliband

et al., eds., *Socialist Register, 1987* (London: The Merlin Press, 1987), 202.

11. The growth in the unemployment of labor was disguised for some time by the establishment of educational retraining programs connected with the "war on poverty." As mentioned in Chapter 1, the growing underemployment of capital—as reflected in the falling capacity utilization rate—began in 1966. Since 1966, the Fed has engaged in a number of revisions of capacity utilization data in an effort to minimize the recorded underemployment of capital.

12. The true Japanese unemployment rate is apparently much higher than the 2 to 3 percent figure usually cited. According to the *Wall Street Journal*, 9 April 1979, "some labor experts estimate that as many as 6 million—12 percent of the labor force—are unemployed or the equivalent of unemployed, which means that workers are paid salaries without having a productive job in the economy." The Japanese female labor force participation rate, although declining in the mid-seventies, has apparently stabilized, or is even increasing slightly. See *The Japan Economic Journal*, 14 September 1985, 3.

13. An added advantage of the exodus from the home may lie in the professionalization of early child care rather than the passing along of antiquated family practices, such as spanking. I suspect that child battery may also be reduced by giving more women the option of turning over early child care to professionals. Indirect evidence of the presence of covert unemployment in the home is provided by the growth of the cult of daytime soap operas.

14. While the armed services have been progressive in their treatment of minorities and women, they have been particularly adamant about ferreting out homosexuals from their ranks. The General Accounting Office, in a study initiated by California Congresswomen Barbara Boxer and the late Sala Burton, estimated that the military's anti-gay exclusionary policy led to the waste of $23 million in training in 1983 alone after the dismissal of about 1,800 gay service members, plus another $370,000 to process these military discharges. During the preceding decade, almost 115,000 service men and women were discharged, with the trend upward. In 1987, 68 Marines were discharged for homosexuality, down from 88 in 1986, 105 in 1985, and 116 in 1984. The United States Navy accounts for over half of the total. As a result of the armed services screening of new recruits for AIDS after 1985, we might expect the costs of this program to fall. See *The Advocate*, 27 November 1984, 8, and *The New York Times*, 23

February 1988, A-23. As we shall see in Chapter 6, there has been no positive competition from the Russians in this area since 1934. Nor is there positive competition in the use of Soviet women (other than nurses) in the armed forces, although there have been rumors that the drafting of Soviet women was being contemplated because of the severe labor shortages of the 1980s. Young women between the ages of fifteen and eighteen were drafted beginning in 1940, but military training for young women was abolished by a decree of August 13, 1946. During the war, one million women served in the Soviet armed forces. See Mervyn Matthews, *Education in the Soviet Union* (Boston: Allen and Unwin, 1982), 38, 68. Also Mark Harrison, *Soviet Planning in Peace and War* (Cambridge: Cambridge University Press, 1986), 137. The East Germans have accepted female volunteers for officer training. See Dale R. Herspring, "The Military Factor in East German Soviet Policy," *Slavic Review* (Spring 1988), 102.

15. W. E. B. DuBois expressed the black community's resentment of universal military training, especially if segregation continued, arguing for the election of Wallace since the "draft will only continue the semislavery of the American Negro." *Chicago Defender*, 7 February 1948, as reproduced by Herbert Aptheker, ed., *Newspaper Columns of W. E. B. DuBois* (White Plains, NY: Kraus-Thomson, 1986), 761.

16. Leo Nichols, *Breakthrough on the Color Front* (New York: Random House, 1953), 205.

17. See Curtis D. MacDougall, *Gideon's Army* (New York: Marzani and Munsell, 1965), 388, 480, 667, 850.

18. David W. Southern, *Gunnar Myrdal and Black-White Relations: The Use and Abuse of An American Dilemma, 1944–1969* (Baton Rouge, LA: Louisiana State University Press, 1987), 49, 50, 74, 293.

19. *Amsterdam News*, 7 August 1943, as reprinted in: Herbert Aptheker, ed., *Newspaper Columns*, 544.

20. Edward Hallett Carr, *The Soviet Impact on the Western World* (New York: Macmillan, 1947), 44–45.

21. *One-Third of a Nation, A Report of The Commission on Minority Participation in Education and American Life*, American Council on Education, Washington, D.C., May 1988, 18.

22. For one thing, a victory for the "right to life" approach to childbirth would no doubt result in a deterioration in our infant mortality figures, which already lag behind other advanced capitalist countries. According to Michael Grossman et al., of the National Bureau of

Economic Research, the single most important factor in reducing the neonatal mortality rate "among blacks and whites over the past two decades has been the wider availability of abortion." See Alan L. Otten, "Slowing Drop in Infant Death Rate Fuels Debate on U.S. Spending for Child, Maternal Problems," *Wall Street Journal*, 23 July 1985, 64. United States sovietologists frequently contrast our declining infant mortality rates with rising infant mortality in the USSR after 1973. A large share of the rise in infant mortality rates in the USSR can be explained as the result of a weighting problem. Infant mortality continued to fall in the RSFSR, Ukraine, Belorussia, and the three Baltic Republics. But a higher percentage of all births take place in Central Asia, where infant mortality is higher, and statistics in earlier years failed to account for all infant mortality, particularly stillbirths. Moslem resistance to abortion undoubtedly contributed to these rates.

23. Thomas Sowell, *Markets and Minorities*, 105; also Michael Reich, *Racial Inequality: A Political Economic Analysis* (Princeton: Princeton University Press, 1981).

24. Margaret E. Leahy, *Development Strategies and the Status of Women* (Boulder, CO: Lynne Rienner, 1986), 23.

25. David W. Southern, *Gunnar Myrdal*, 62. On the exclusion of black women from WPA projects, see Cecilia A. Conrod, "When and Where I Enter," *The Review of Black Political Economy* (Fall-Winter 1985–86), 66–67.

26. Herbert Aptheker, ed., *Newspaper Columns*, 105. For an account of the positive role of Frances Perkins, see Eileen Boris and Michael Honey, "Gender, Race, and Politics of the Labor Department," *Monthly Labor Review*, February 1988, 29.

27. Joel Williamson, *The Crucible of Race: Black-White Relations in the American South Since Emancipation* (New York: Oxford University Press, 1984). Myrdal in *An American Dilemma* claims that there was a slight upturn in black net reproductive rates relative to whites by 1940.

28. George M. Fredrickson, "Panic in the South," *New York Review of Books*, 6 December 1984, 28. This attitude towards blacks was reflected in the notorious Tuskegee Syphilis Experiment, initiated in 1932. In this study, the United States Public Health Service conducted an experiment on 600 poor and uneducated black males with tertiary stage syphilis. No treatment was provided for forty years, despite the use of penicillin beginning in 1942. This use of human

guinea pigs mirrored the human experiments of fascist Germany and Japan. See Jean Heller, "Syphilis Victims in U.S. Study Went Untreated for 40 Years," *The New York Times*, 26 July 1972, 1. See also H. James Jones, *Bad Blood* (New York: The Free Press, 1981). According to Myrdal in *Dilemma* (174, 1225), black draftees in World War II were thirteen times more likely to have syphilis than whites, and there were proportionally more childless women in the black population.

29. William Julius Wilson, *The Declining Significance of Race* (Chicago: University of Chicago Press, 1980), 62.

30. Thomas Cripps, *Slow Fade to Black* (New York: Oxford University Press, 1977), 106. Blacks became the first victims of the rollback of production during the decade of the Great Depression.

Chapter 3

1. Jack D. Foner, *Blacks and the Military in American History: A New Perspective* (New York: Praeger, 1974), 15. A serious Soviet account of black participation in the American Revolutionary War and Russian pre-revolutionary support for American blacks can be found in Robert Ivanov, *Blacks in United States History* (Moscow: Progress, 1985). This well-intentioned book is a good example of Soviet NFL thinking: "No one has ever been able to solve the problem of both guns and butter" (p. 190). According to Ivanov, who cites Victor Perlo, the Chair of the Economic Commission of the Communist Party, U.S.A., "white workers around the country are paid many tens of billions of dollars less than they should be because of the super-exploitation of Blacks" (p. 211). There is no mention of United States affirmative action programs or white capitalist support of these policies. It should be mentioned that the Communist Party, U.S.A. and its race expert, Herbert Aptheker, have strongly supported affirmative action in recent years. See *Black Law Journal*, 1987, and Marvin J. Berlowitz and Carol E. Morgan, editors, *Racism, Imperialism, and Peace* (Minneapolis: MEP Publications, 1987), 157–62.

2. Martin Binkin and Mark J. Eitelberg, *Blacks and the Military* (Washington, D.C.: The Brookings Institution, 1982), 15.

3. Bernard C. Nalty, *Strength for the Fight: A History of Black Americans in the Military* (New York: The Free Press, 1986), 141.

4. Citizens' Commission on Civil Rights, *Affirmative Action to*

Open the Door of Job Opportunity: A Policy of Fairness and Compassion That Has Worked (Washington, D.C., 1984). This source is absolutely essential to understanding the positive position on affirmative action taken by members of the Citizens' Commission including, among others, such illustrious citizens as Arthur S. Flemming, Erwin Griswold, Theodore Hesburgh, Eleanor Holmes Norton, Elliot Richardson, and Ray Marshall. A great deal of the following material is contained in this important source.

5. The positive impact of employment-creating FL institutions (such as reparations in Table 1 above) was also seen in Europe at about the same time. The end of the Franco-German War in 1871 put a reparations "burden" on France amounting to about $5 billion. As a result of the actual payment of this reparations bill, the French economy prospered, and the German economy, which was forced to accept the reparations, was subject to grave economic difficulties. Writing in the first decade of this century, Norman Angell complained that paradoxically, "by any test that you care to apply, France, the vanquished, is better off than Germany, the victor. . . . The French people are as a whole more prosperous, more comfortable, more economically secure, with a greater reserve of savings than are the Germans. . . . There is something wrong with a financial operation that gives these results." See Norman Angell, *The Great Illusion: A Study of the Relation of Military Power to National Advantage* (London: G. P. Putnam's Sons Publisher, 1914), 91.

6. Unemployment in Massachusetts during this period is the subject of Alexander Keyssar's *The First Century of Unemployment in Massachusetts* (New York: Cambridge University Press, 1986).

7. For a good discussion of the early sexist position of the AF of L, see Bettina Berch, *The Endless Day* (New York: Harcourt Brace Jovanovich, 1982), 41–48. For an account of the racist position of early trade unions dominated by recently arrived white ethnic groups from Europe, see Ross and Hill, *Employment*, 31–82. As a result, black workers increasingly perceived the discriminatory behavior of labor unions as a conspiracy by foreigners.

8. Bradley R. Schiller, *The Economics of Poverty and Discrimination* (Englewood Cliffs, NJ: Prentice-Hall, 1984), 156.

9. For a discussion of the relationship between blacks and the Communist party, see Harvard Sitkoff, *A New Deal for Blacks: The Emergence of Civil Rights as a National Issue* (New York: Oxford,

1978), especially 139–68. Also, Robert Allen, *Black Awakening in Capitalist America* (Garden City, NY: Doubleday, 1969).

10. The depression of the 1870s was followed by the Chinese Exclusion Act of 1882, which prohibited the immigration of additional Chinese workers for a decade. See Jan Wong, "Bias Against Orientals Increases the Rivalry of Nations' Economies," *Wall Street Journal*, 28 November 1986, 1. The thrust of this account of recent discrimination against Asians is that the trade imbalance with Japan has resulted in a resurgence of Asia-bashing. Also see Ross and Hill, *Employment*, 41–43.

11. In the words of Sally Miller, "The Socialist Party remained as invisible to the Negroes as the Negro was invisible to the Party." See her "Socialism and Race," in: John H. M. Laslett and Seymour Martin Lipset, eds., *Failure of a Dream?* (Berkeley: University of California Press, 1974), 228.

12. There were no blacks involved in the formation of the United States Communist Party after World War I, and it required the intervention of Lenin in 1921 before the party undertook organizational work among blacks. By 1938, 14 percent of the party members were black. See Robert L. Allen, *Reluctant Reformers: Racism and Social Reform Movements in the United States* (Washington, D.C.: Howard University Press, 1974), 226. Also see William Z. Foster, *The Negro People in America* (New York: International Publishers, 1954), 455 and Theodore Draper, *American Communism and Soviet Russia* (New York: Octagon Books, 1977), 321.

13. Margaret E. Leahy, *Development Strategies*, 27.

14. Bernard C. Nalty, *Strength for the Fight*, 130.

15. Bradley R. Schiller, *Economics of Poverty*, 214–15. For a detailed account of the treatment of blacks in the Depression, see John B. Kirby, *Black Americans in the Roosevelt Era* (Knoxville: University of Tennessee Press, 1980).

16. As a result of ghettoization, it has been possible for blacks to achieve some political representation in the House of Representatives and in some central cities, although not in the Senate or as governors of states.

17. This was one of the very few instances in which the United States Communist party—which was more concerned with the survival of the USSR—failed to support black protests. See Ross and Hill, *Employment*, 74.

Chapter 4

1. Lee Nichols, *Breakthrough on the Color Front* (New York: Random House, 1953), 41.

2. The last segregated units disappeared from the army by October 31, 1954. See Leo Bogart, ed., *Social Research and the Desegregation of the U.S. Army* (Chicago: Markham Publishing, 1969), 321. This is a formerly classified report with a retrospective introduction by Leo Bogart on "Clear," the code name for the research of a civilian "think tank" which led to the official desegregation of the U.S. Army during the Korean conflict. According to Bernard C. Nalty, *Strength for the Fight*, 254, "the reforms did come to pass, but they were more the product of the demand for manpower created by a war in the Far East than a result of Fahy's reasoned argument." The replacement of General MacArthur by the nonracist General Matthew Ridgway was also an important development in the integration of the army in Korea.

3. The same can be said for some private Catholic church schools in the South, which were integrated before the Supreme Court decision in 1954.

4. There was a certain amount of fear of "tipping points" or "overrepresentation"—that the armed forces would become predominantly black—with the result that armed forces recruitment has become more selective with respect to blacks than to whites. In the early 1980s, 95.4 percent of young blacks joining the army had high school diplomas, compared to only 87.6 percent of young whites entering. See Charles C. Moskos, "Success Story: Blacks in the Army," *The Atlantic Monthly*, May 1986, 67. According to Moskos, "today's army enlisted ranks is the only arena in American society where black educational levels surpass those of whites and by a significant degree." See Charles C. Moskos, "How to Save the All-Volunteer Force," *The Public Interest* 61 (Fall 1980), 77. The same can be said for women, since only women with a high school degree are eligible for recruitment.

5. Charles C. Moskos, "Success Story," 64.

6. The linking of this decision to the Cold War was not lost on blacks, according to James Baldwin, *The Fire Next Time* (New York: Dell, 1962), 111. "Most of the Negroes I know do not believe that this immense concession [*Brown v. Board of Education*] would have ever been made if it had not been for the competition of the Cold War,

and the fact that Africa was clearly liberating herself and therefore had, for practical reasons, to be wooed by the descendants of her former masters."

7. Lynchings of blacks by whites were common for the first time between 1890 and 1915. Before 1890, most lynchings occurred on the Western frontier, and most victims were white. Suddenly, lynchings became "a distinctly interracial happening in the South." In the 1890s, an average of 138 people were lynched yearly in the South, of whom 75 percent were blacks. Between 1885 and 1907, there were more lynchings in the United States than there were legal executions. See Joel Williamson, *The Crucible of Race: Black-White Relations in the American South Since Emancipation* (New York: Oxford University Press, 1984). Lynchings of blacks in the South were also very common in the period before World War II and in the early postwar years, when they were frequently the subject of critical comment by Soviet propagandists. State Department officials estimated at the time that about half of Soviet propaganda focused on the United States racial situation, according to David W. Southern, *Gunnar Myrdal*, 102. Also, Anatol Rapoport, *Science and the Goals of Man* (New York: Harper and Row, 1950), 46–47, as included in: Harry G. Shaffer, ed., *The Soviet System in Theory and Practice* (New York: Frederick Ungar, 1984), 233.

8. Walter Goodman, "Pace of Executions in U.S. Quickens," *The New York Times*, 25 November 1984, 4. In at least one Texas case, a stay of execution was requested by a white man on the grounds that proportionately more white men were being executed.

9. The Supreme Court heard and rejected arguments in *McClesky v. Kemp* that in Georgia from 1973 to 1979, murderers of white men were eleven times more likely to receive the death penalty than murderers of blacks. See John B. Judis, "The Black and White of Capital Punishment," *In These Times*, 5–11 November 1986, 3.

10. Bernard C. Nalty, *Strength for the Fight*, 274.

11. On January 18, 1973, the United States District Court of Philadelphia approved a consent decree in which AT&T agreed to revise its promotion and job transfer practices, to make changes in testing procedures, and to pay $38 million in back pay, a figure later increased to $80 million. For an account of legal challenges by two AFL-CIO unions that delayed implementation of an affirmative action program, see Ross and Hill, *Employment*, 65.

12. At Yale University, Jewish undergraduate enrollment was

limited to about 10 percent of the total student population until 1960. By 1986, Jewish students accounted for about 30 percent of the total. See *The New York Times*, 9 March 1986, E-6. See also Dan A. Oren, *Joining the Club* (New Haven: Yale University Press, 1986).

13. For a detailed answer to these charges, see *Report*, 148–71. See also John Edwards, *Positive Discrimination, Social Justice, and Social Policy: Moral Scrutiny of a Policy Practice* (London: Tavistock, 1987).

14. Examples of the effects of "heightism" can be found in: Dennis D. Miller, "Is It Height or Sex Discrimination?" *Challenge*, September-October 1986, 59–61.

15. According to *The New York Times*, 23 February 1986, 28, their proposal to abolish affirmative action requirements "has run into strong resistance, not only from civil rights groups, but from Labor Secretary Bill Brock and six other cabinet members, 69 Senators, the Republican leaders in both the House and the Senate, some Jewish groups, the National Association of Manufacturers, and many large companies. They say that affirmative action has been good for business as well as nonwhites and women who might not otherwise have had a chance to develop their potential." It is perhaps significant that the United States Chamber of Commerce, which tends to represent small businessmen, refused to sign. However, Stephen Boskat, vice-president and general counsel of the chamber, reacted favorably to the Supreme Court decision in *Johnson v. Santa Clara County Transportation Agency*, declaring that it reduced "fear of a reverse discrimination suit"—something which represents a greater threat to small businessmen. See *The New York Times*, 29 March 1987, sec. 4, 1. Vice-President George Bush, in his address to the NAACP convention, claimed that "he always has and always will support affirmative action programs to help blacks get and keep jobs." *San Jose Mercury News*, 13 July 1988, A-11.

16. Andrew Hacker, "Women Vs. Men in the Work Force," *New York Times Magazine*, 9 December 1984, 124–29.

17. See *Ms.*, June 1987, 64–65.

18. *The New York Times*, 25 November 1984, 4.

19. From 1970 to 1986, the percentage of blacks earning over $50,000 (1986 dollars) increased by 87 percent, while the percentage of whites earning over $50,000 yearly increased by only 49 percent. See *The New York Times*, 29 February 1988, B-8. At the same time, the percentage of blacks earning less than $5,000 yearly increased from 9.6 percent to 14.0 percent, while the percentage for

whites increased from 3.1 to 3.5 percent.

20. A RAND study published in February 1986, shows black male income in 1980 at 72.6 percent of white male income, compared to only 57.5 percent in 1960. See *The New York Times*, 2 March 1986, E-8.

21. Carl Siciliano, "Racial Segregation Renewed," *The Catholic Worker*, September 1987, 1.

22. Commission on Minority Participation in Education and American Life, *One-Third of a Nation*, 11–13. Black women have held their own from 1976–86, accounting for 5.1% of college enrollment in 1976 and 5.2% a decade later. During these same years, black men fell from 4.3% to 3.5% of the total. See *The New York Times*, 17 January 1989, A-23.

23. *A Dream Deferred: The Economic Status of Black Americans*, a working paper by the Center for the Study of Social Policy, Washington, July 1983, 31. Nationally, blacks were 2.4 times as likely as whites to be unemployed in 1987. The worst city was Milwaukee, with 25.9 percent black unemployment, and a 5.1:1 ratio of black to white unemployment rates. See *San Francisco Chronicle*, 14 July 1987, 2.

Chapter 5

1. Only seventy-eight thousand labor force participants (out of a total of twelve million) replied by writing in "black" as a description of their ethnic origin, which is undoubtedly an underestimate of the Canadian black population. In the 1986 census, "black" was added to the ethnic groups specifically listed. See *Report of the Commission on Equality in Employment*, 1984, 53, hereafter referred to as *Report*. In Toronto, where about half of Canada's black population resides, blacks account for almost 4 percent of the total population. They have unemployment rates which are only slightly higher than the general population and have incomes that are 75 to 80 percent of the average in the city. See Ph.D. dissertation of Carl E. James, "The Challenge of Making It: Youth's Career Aspirations and Perceptions of Their Chances to Achieve" (York University, April 1986).

2. This view has been challenged by Reynolds Farley of The Population Studies Center of the University of Michigan. Working with 1980 census data, Farley finds that foreign-born black males earned slightly less than native black males. See his unpublished paper, "Race, Ancestry, and Socioeconomic Status: Are Foreign-Born

Blacks More Successful?" The exclusion of second and third generation Caribbean blacks from Farley's data may account for differences
between Sowell's and Farley's conclusions.

3. Reverse penetration of ideas is rare. Despite the highly successful socialized medical system of Canada, the United States remains
committed to high-cost private medicine and insurance, with
Medicaid for the indigent. As a result, United States residents of
northern border states frequently cross the border to take advantage
of less expensive medical services in Canada.

4. *Report*, 22.

5. *The New York Times*, 25 November 1984, 32.

6. *Economic Report of the President*, 1987, 221. The temporary
decline in the 1960s is attributed to the sudden entry of liberated
women with less than average education and experience. In this fas-
cinating chapter, all credit for improvement of women's lot in the
United States is given to the working of the market, and there is no
mention of affirmative action, the women's movement, or the pill—a
marvelous example of the myopia of Reaganaut economists. The
Equal Pay Act of 1963 and Title VII of the Civil Rights Act of 1964
are mentioned in passing. Weekly earnings of full-time female
workers in 1987 were 70 percent of male earnings, according to
Eileen Boris and Michael Honey, in *Monthly Labor Review*, February
1988, 34.

7. For the United States, the unexplained differential between the
hourly earnings of male and female physicians in 1982 was 12 to 13
percent. See Robert L. Ohsfeldt and Steven D. Culler, "Differences
in Income Between Male and Female Physicians," *Journal of Health
Economics* (June 1987), 1–12.

8. *The Globe and Mail* (Toronto), 29 March 1985, 2.

9. Recessions tend to hit the goods-producing industries as opposed to the service sector, which may actually grow during these
years. Since men are working predominantly in the goods-producing
sectors subject to recessions, their unemployment rates grow more
than proportionately.

10. *Economic Report of the President*, 1987, 216.

11. *The New York Times*, 25 November 1984, 84.

12. See Sylvia Hewlett, *A Lesser Life: The Myth of Women's Liberation in America* (New York: William Morrow, 1986), 237, 279. By
1945, one hundred thousand children were enrolled in United States
federally supported facilities. There was a small federal appropriation

for child care in 1962, the first since World War II, but this was cut out of the 1965 budget—additional evidence that full employment was not a characteristic of the Vietnam War. Forty-one percent of Canadian mothers of children under six held jobs in 1976 as compared to over 60 percent in 1986. Still, only a handful of companies offered child care. See *Maclean's*, 10 November 1986, 52. Also Tanis Day, "Historical Causes of Occupational Segregation," a paper prepared for Western Economic Association meetings in Vancouver, B. C., July 1987.

13. Nestor Cruz, "Is Equal Employment Opportunity Cost Effective?" *Labor Law Review* 5 (May 1980), 295, as cited in *Report*, 18.

14. *Report*, 7. For a detailed, negative reaction to the Abella Report, see Walter Block and Michael A. Walker, *On Employment Equity* (Vancouver, B.C.: The Fraser Institute, 1985).

15. *Report*, 10.

16. *The Globe and Mail*, 2 March 1985, 4, and 9 March 1985, 2.

17. *Wall Street Journal*, 27 May 1986, 26. Some sharp improvements were recorded by Australia, another signer, where women's wages rose from 65 percent of male earnings in 1970 to 87 percent by 1977, but fell back to 82 percent by 1982. Ireland, the United Kingdom, and Switzerland also reported short-term gains in closing the wage gap. In the United States, Clarence M. Pendleton, Jr., Chairman of the United States Civil Rights Commission, characterized comparable worth as "the looniest idea since Looney Tunes came on the screen." The Reagan administration and federal courts have also tended to reject the idea of comparable worth. Nevertheless, thirteen states have begun to adjust their employees' pay, at least partly on the basis of this idea. Mainstream economists have tended to reject this concept, just as they have traditionally rejected minimum wage legislation. See "States Leading on Pay Equity," *The New York Times*, 22 June 1987, D-2. However, see Barbara Bergman, "Pay Equity—Surprising Answers to Hard Questions," *Challenge*, May-June 1987, 45–51.

18. Compare Pat Spencer, "Discrimination By Decree," *The Body Politic*, April 1985, 9, and *The New York Times*, 17 April 1985, A-12. A discussion paper issued by John C. Crosbie, Canada's Justice Minister, suggested that section 15 of the Charter may be interpreted by the courts to be "open-ended" and may eventually be interpreted to guarantee the rights of homosexuals and other groups who were not initially named. Subsequently, Canada moved to ban mandatory retirement of civil servants at sixty-five, to allow (overt) homosexuals

to serve in their armed forces and the Royal Canadian Mounted Police, and to permit women to assume combat duties in the air force. See Christopher S. Wren, "Canada Seeks to End Discrimination in Jobs," *The New York Times*, 9 March 1986, 6.

19. Douglas Martin, "Canadians Celebrate a New Charter of Rights," *The New York Times*, 17 April 1985, A-12.

20. Clyde Haberman, "Japan's Women Win Scuffle in Equality War," *The New York Times*, 18 May 1985, 1.

21. *Vestnik Statistiki* 1 (1987), 57. The highest female student percentage is for Sweden (56 percent). The USSR is runner up with 55.4 percent.

22. For a good discussion of sexist British laws, see Joann S. Lublin, "In Britain, Women May Lead But Sexism Rules," *Wall Street Journal*, 13 March 1987, 24. In contrast to Britain, where Prime Minister Thatcher opposes affirmative action, Norway's feminist prime minister has increased the role of women in top government posts.

23. The German Democratic Republic encourages part-time work, and there is legislation granting workers (usually women) the right to one paid day off monthly for household chores.

24. Sylvia Hewlett, *A Lesser Life*. The Federal Republic's child-care policy for under-threes is even poorer than that of the United States. See Sheila B. Kamerman and Alfred J. Kahn, *Child Care, Family Benefits, and Working Parents* (New York: Columbia University Press, 1981), 87.

25. Judith Miller, "Politics an Uphill Fight for French Women," *The New York Times*, 15 March 1986, 50.

26. It was not until 1987 that Britain elected its first black member of Parliament.

27. Gavin M. Chen, "Minority Business Development: An International Comparison," *The Review of Black Political Economy* (Fall 1986), 104–108.

Chapter 6

1. See my "What's So Attractive About Marxism-Leninism?" *Coexistence* 5 (January 1968), 223–27. Also "Is the Soviet Union Really an Imperialistic Power?" *Contemporary Crises* (April 1978), 157–66.

2. See Ralph Miliband, "Freedom, Democracy and the American Alliance," in: Ralph Miliband et al., *Socialist Register 1987* (London:

The Merlin Press, 1987), 490. According to Miliband, "the real problem, for the United States and its allies, is to be found . . . in the fact that the Soviet Union does provide a measure of military, economic, and political support to revolutionary regimes; and this in some cases has been crucial for their capacity to resist American attempts to destabilize and destroy them." This is the Soviet "threat" rather than any Soviet "expansionist ambitions."

3. W. Arthur Lewis, *Racial Conflict*, 52.

4. David W. Southern, *Gunnar Myrdal*, xiii.

5. At the time of the first Soviet Constitution, the Ukraine, the Caucasus, Central Asia, Siberia, and other former Russian territories were under enemy occupation; hence, the term "Russian Socialist Federation Soviet Republic."

6. Before the Senate finally approved the convention in 1986 by a vote of 83 to 11, Senator Proxmire called the thirty-seven years of inaction "one of the most useful propaganda clubs the Soviet Union has ever had." See Robert Toner, "After 37 Years, Senate Endorses a Genocide Ban," *The New York Times*, 20 February 1986, A-4.

7. See *Soviet News*, 20 March 1985, 107.

8. Michael Ellman, *Collectivizations*, 182. See also Alec Nove and J. A. Newth, *The Soviet Middle East: A Communist Model for Development* (London 1967), 46; Charles K. Wilbur, *The Soviet Model and Underdeveloped Countries* (Chapel Hill: University of North Carolina Press, 1969); and Philippe J. Bernard, *Planning in the Soviet Union* (Oxford: Pergamon Press, 1966), 213.

9. Michael Ellman, *Collectivization*, 209. Water charges for cotton growing in the early years were also one-half those for other users, according to William Mandel, *Environment*, May 1973. As producers of citrus and other exotic fruit (pomegranates, mandarin oranges, etc.) sold at farmers' markets, the farmers of Central Asia and the Transcaucasus have frequently marketed their produce at very high prices in northern urban areas.

10. Robert Conquest, ed., *The Last Empire: Nationality and the Soviet Future* (Stanford: Hoover University Press, 1986), 308. See also Patrick Cockburn, "Dateline USSR: Ethnic Tremors," *Foreign Policy*, Spring 1989, 172.

11. William Mandel, *Soviet But Not Russian* (Edmonton, Canada: University of Alberta Press, 1985), 76.

12. Unemployment compensation was eliminated in 1930, but as many as 100,000 structurally unemployed have been unoffi-

cially reported as late as 1939.

13. The Crimean Tatars (accounting for 500,000 Soviet citizens) were only fully rehabilitated as a nation in 1967, but were prohibited from returning to their historic homeland in the Crimea. For Andropov's role in this discriminatory policy, see Zhores Medvedev, *Andropov* (New York: W. W. Norton and Co., 1983), 85–86. A good account of Soviet discrimination against these groups can be found in Isabelle Kreindler, "The Soviet Deported Nationalities: A Summary and Update," *Soviet Studies* (July 1986), 387–405. For an extensive account of the problems of the Crimean Tatars and their resistance, see Ludmilla Alexeyeva, *Soviet Dissent* (Middletown, CT: Wesleyan University Press, 1987), 137–59. In July 1987, large numbers of Tatars demonstrated in Red Square, after which they were received by Andrei Gromyko.

14. Early suffrage for Russian women actually began under the fragile Kerensky regime in March 1917. This was used by suffragettes in pressuring President Wilson to extend political democracy to United States women. As noted in the *Miami Daily Metropole* of 30 June 1917: "It is ludicrous for Washington diplomats to pose as teachers of democracy to the people of benighted Russia which had admitted the women of their country to equal political civil rights with men." See Christine A. Lunarduri, *From Equal Suffrage to Equal Rights* (New York: New York University Press, 1986), 126.

15. *Soviet Education,* May-June 1984, 7.

16. The first census was not published because Stalin found it difficult to believe that so few citizens remained after collectivization and the drought. The second census, more or less confirming the first, appeared two years later in 1939. Legalized abortion began to be restricted as early as 1935, according to Frank Lorimer, *The Population of the Soviet Union: History and Prospects* (Geneva: League of Nations, 1946), 128.

17. Albert Szymanski estimates that the ratio of legal abortions to live births in the United States is one-sixth the Soviet rate. Albert Szymanski, *Human Rights in the Soviet Union* (London: Zed, 1984), 110. In 1978–79, the number of abortions per thousand women in the reproductive ages was 27.5 in the United States. It was 102.4 in the USSR, 123.2 in the RSFSR, 68.3 in Bulgaria, 36.9 in Hungary, 28.9 in Czechoslovakia, and only 5.9 in the FRG. See *Current Digest of the Soviet Press,* 2 December 1987, 15.

18. The divorce rate is higher in the German Democratic Republic

than it is in the Federal Republic of Germany, presumably as a reflection of greater liberation of women in the East. Divorce is also more frequently initiated by GDR women, as in other countries, including the USSR.

19. Vladimir Mezhenkov, ed., *Soviet Scene 1987* (Moscow: Progress, 1987), 99.

20. David Lane, *The End of Equality*, 88–89, as cited by Branko Horvat, *Political Economy of Socialism*, 75. Horvat, writing critically of "etatism" in the Soviet Union and Eastern Europe, recognizes that upward mobility of workers and women represents important positive changes. See also Genio Browning, "Soviet Politics: Where Are The Women?" in: Barbara Holland, ed., *Soviet Sisterhood* (Bloomington: Indiana University Press, 1985), 207.

21. Szymanski, *Human Rights*, 119–20.

22. See ECE *Report on Women*, 22. The Canadian figures may be misleading due to the inclusion in Quebec of students in three-year junior colleges starting at the senior level of high school.

23. *Soviet Education* (May-June 1984), 19. Central Asia still graduates 50 to 100 percent more men than women, and the gap actually worsened between 1959 and 1970 in Azerbaijan, Tadzikistan, and Turkmenia. See George Avis, "Access to Higher Education in the Soviet Union in the 1980s," in: J. J. Tomiak, *Soviet Education in the 1980s* (London: Croom Helm, 1983), 209. See also Barbara A. Anderson, "The Life Course of Soviet Women Born 1905–1960," in: James R. Millar, ed., *Politics, Work, and Daily Life in the USSR* (Cambridge: Cambridge University Press, 1987). According to her sample of Soviet women, Anderson concludes that the differential between female and male earnings is not as great for Soviet European cities as it is in the United States.

24. See William Moskoff, "An Estimate of the Soviet Male-Female Income Differential," *ACES Bulletin*, Fall 1974, 24. Soviet sampling of the relationship between the incomes of males and females in the same family comes up with highly divergent results. One source claims that only 15 percent of Soviet women earn as much as their mates; the other that 79 percent earn as much or more than their husbands. See Joel C. Moses, *The Politics of Women and Work in the Soviet Union and the United States* (Berkeley: Institute of International Studies, 1983), 154. Gail Lapidus estimates that Soviet women make 65 to 70 percent of male earnings, in: Jennie Farley, ed., *Women Workers in 15 Countries* (Ithaca: ILR Press, 1986), 20.

25. Szymanski, *Human Rights*, 116.

26. The lifetime earnings gap is minimized by a number of factors: women receive five more years of pension and have an edge of ten years of longer life expectancy. They are also not required to serve in the armed forces at low pay for two years. In 1979, a Soviet recruit earned 3.80 rubles per month, compared with a minimum wage of 70 rubles per month. See Tom Gervasi, *The Myth of Soviet Military Supremacy* (New York: Harper and Row, 1986).

27. The Soviet magazine, *Smena*, cites a study indicating that a working woman's reward for getting married is an extra fifteen hours housework per week. See "Sex and the Soviet Girl," *The Economist*, 12 October 1985, 64. In the United States, men actually demand eight hours more service weekly than they contribute. See Heidi Hartman, "The Family as the Locus of Gender, Class, and Political Struggle," *Signs* (Spring 1981), 383.

28. See *Ekonomika Sovetskoi Ukrainy* 1 (1984), 94, as cited in: V. Mikhailuk, "Ways of Increasing the Social Effectiveness of Women's Labor," *Problems of Economics* (January 1986), 65. In Hungary, in 1977, the average Hungarian woman spent 4.5 hours in the household daily, compared to 2.5 hours per man; in 1963, the figures were 5 and 2 hours, respectively. See Janos Timar, "Employment Policy in Hungary," in Jan Adam, ed., *Employment Policy in Hungary* (London: Macmillan, 1987), 113.

29. Fred Weir, "Tearing Off a Hidden Veil," *Canadian Tribune*, 2 May 1988, 6.

30. It is possible that the Soviet change of policy may have been influenced by the rise of Hitler and his draconian policy with respect to homosexuals. As mentioned above, "opposing forces frequently tend to take on each other's characteristics, both positive and negative." For an account of Hitler's treatment of gays, see James D. Steakley, *The Homosexual Emancipation Movement in Germany* (New York: Arno Press, 1975), especially chapter 4, "The Final Solution, 1933–45," 103–19.

31. In 1984, when I visited Tbilisi, I learned that Paradzhanov had been rehabilitated and had just completed his first postprison film, *Suram Fortress*. For an account of discrimination against lesbians in the "prosperous" Baltic Republics, see Inessa Tominaite, "The Right to be Myself," in: Tatyana Mamonova, ed., *Women and Russia* (Boston: Beacon Press, 1984), 145–49.

32. See Alexeyeva, *Soviet Dissent*, chapters 11–13.

33. See Howard L. Parsons, *Christianity Today in the USSR* (New York: International Publishers, 1987), 13–14. According to Parsons, "Antireligious propaganda was greatly stepped up through the schools, Houses of Culture, lectures, books, and the Society for the Dissemination of Political and Scientific Knowledge, which revived the work of the defunct League of Militant Atheists." It is estimated that up to half of the churches previously operating may have been closed.

34. Ludmilla Alexeyeva, *Soviet Dissent*, 45.

35. See exchange between William Mandel and Marshall Goldman in *Environment*, December 1972, and May and October 1973. See also William Mandel, "The Soviet Energy Movement," *Science and Society* (Winter 1972), 385–416. Also, Robert McIntyre and J. Thornton, "Environmental Divergence: Air Pollution in the USSR," *Journal of Environmental Economics and Management* 1:2 (August 1974), 109–20. The volume of air pollutants emitted in Moscow had declined by 1967 to one-third the 1960 level.

36. In 1953, the problem of forest conservation was placed under the same administrator who was responsible for the production of lumber. It remained that way until 1966, when a separate cabinet level forestry agency was established. See William Mandel, "Environment, USSR," *New World Review* 41:1 (1973), 78–80. As of 1987, there were seven organizations, each of which had its own approach to environmental protection. Soviet media were arguing for a single state body dealing with environmental problems. See Gena Kovalov, "Environmental Concerns in the Soviet Union," *People's Daily World*, 12 August 1987, A-9.

37. As late as 1986, pollution of Lake Baikal continues, according to *The Current Digest of the Soviet Press*, 12 February 1986, 12. Also Gena Kovalov, *ibid*. Pollution is coming from the new cities built along the Baikal-Amur Railway (BAM).

38. *Izvestiia*, 18 January 1987.

39. See D. Richard Little, "Mass Political Participation in the U.S. and the USSR," *Comparative Political Studies* 8:4 (January 1976), as included in Harry G. Shaffer, *The Soviet System*, 244. "Protection of nature is a most widespread form of voluntary activity in the country. For example, the All-Russia Society for the Protection of Nature numbers some thirty-five million members." See Oleg Yanitsky, "The

Socialist Town: Protection of the Environment of the Population," *Social Science* 4 (1985), 78.

40. There were two occasions during my Fulbright lectures at Moscow State University in the fall of 1978 when I thought I was skating on thin ice: once when I criticized the space race as a great waste of resources, and again when I expressed doubts on the safety of nuclear power. See my *The Advanced Capitalist System* (Armonk, NY: M.E. Sharpe, 1980), 108.

41. Joan De Bardeleben claims that "the range of permissible disagreement and substantive criticism of present (environmental) policies in the popular media is considerably broader in the USSR than in the GDR." See her *The Environment and Marxism-Leninism: The Soviet and East German Experience* (Boulder, CO: Westview Press, 1985), 271.

42. However, see the post-Chernobyl petition of the independent Peace and Ecology Movement and Other Concerned Citizens of the GDR, as reported in: *Labour Focus on Eastern Europe*, November 1986, 36–37.

43. The slowdown in the USSR was also influenced by the delayed effect of the baby bust in the course of World War II and the beginning of the cutback in the official workweek in 1961. For a more complete analysis of the relative role of military spending in the two systems, see my *The Advanced Capitalist System* (Armonk, NY: M.E. Sharpe, 1980), chapter 2 and pp. 113–19.

44. It might be argued that the increase in the announced budget was more of a paper increase designed to strengthen the hands of Soviet arm control negotiators in Geneva. In 1986, the 1985 level of military spending was supposed to continue at this higher level.

Chapter 7

1. See data in Table 2, p. 57, above. The East Germans encourage working women by offering part-time employment possibilities, a day off for housework each month, and reduced workweeks for women with many children. The only significant ethnic minority found in the GDR are the Sorbs, a Slavic minority, who survived the Hitler era and have since been subject to affirmative action legislation in the postwar years. The Sorbs are concentrated in the vicinity of Bautzen, east of Dresden.

2. See Alan Weiss, "The Child Care System in the GDR," *New*

World Review (March-April 1985), 20–22.

3. See Economic Commission for Europe, *Economic Role of Women*, 21.

4. See Harry Shaffer, *Women in the Two Germanies: A Comparative Study of a Socialist and a Non-Socialist Society* (New York: Pergamon Press, 1981). It is no accident that the definitive book on sex education used throughout the socialist world, including Cuba, is a translation of a GDR publication.

5. Both countries would appear to be responsive to the wishes of the majority of their citizenry. If anything, Hungary would appear to be more responsive in soft-pedaling unpopular affirmative action than the USSR, just as Canada is more responsive than the United States. All socialist countries in Eastern Europe have eschewed unemployment compensation since 1930 when the Soviet Union abandoned this institution. At the end of the New Economic Policy, the unemployment rate in Moscow was 20 percent, but, by 1930, the First Five-Year Plan had virtually eliminated the reserve army of unemployed. In 1982, the Hungarians introduced "retraining aid," and in 1985 they reactivated "re-employment aid" for a few hundred persons, which is very similar to unemployment compensation.

6. Janos Timar, *Employment Policy in Hungary*, 105–107.

7. A minister of health during the Stalinist phase, Anna Ratko strictly opposed abortion, thereby producing a baby boom before 1956. There were also pronatalist motives because population growth after 1956—when abortion was legalized, as in the Soviet Union—was insufficient to maintain the total Hungarian population. See Jan Adam, *Employment and Wage Policies in Poland, Czechoslovakia and Hungary Since 1950* (New York: St. Martin's Press, 1984), 52. In addition, the Hungarians agreed to send about fifteen thousand young Hungarian "guest workers" annually to the GDR, where they would receive on-the-job training.

8. The introduction of greater regressivity into these payments in 1985 is in line with the growing popularity of "genetic" approaches to population (such as sperm banks) in Hungary today. Such is the rationale for the comparative lack of special maternity allowances for Gypsy women, for example. Soviet payments for women staying home for one and one-half years after the birth of a child are lower on the average but provide more in relative terms for the poorest—a flat thirty-five rubles per month and fifty rubles per month in Siberia and

other hardship areas. See Gail Lapidus, in Jennie Farley, ed., *Women Workers*, 27.

9. Some East European writers claim that full employment applies only to men and single women—with other women considered to be part of the reserve army of unemployed. See Jan Adam, *Employment and Wage Policies*, 62. The reduction of overt unemployment in West Germany was also used as an argument for the attempted introduction of paid "baby leaves" in the Federal Republic, but the legislation never passed.

10. Polish women were allowed leaves without pay after 1968, according to Jan Adam, *Employment and Wage Policies*, 52.

11. On September 13, 1985, I visited the "Dozsa" collective farm near Veszprem, along with Dr. Jan Adam. Dozsa is an amalgamation of six smaller, independent cooperatives since 1973. The director, Dr. Zoltan Varga, a doctor of agricultural science, stated that the wages of women were 70 percent those of men. Furthermore, although at one time there was a "women's policy" (somewhat equivalent to affirmative action), such was no longer the case.

12. The United States divorce rate was 5 per thousand in 1985, up slightly from 4.9 the previous year. See *The New York Times*, 21 September 1986, 30.

13. As a result, it was reported in 1986 that a group of divorced men in Hungary had organized to pressure for relief.

14. After Chernobyl in April 1986, these limitations on abortion have been relaxed.

15. The conventional total loss is one-half million lives. See "Gypsy Survivors of Nazis Hear Pledge of Aid," *The New York Times*, 17 September 1986, 23. Also, Alexander Ramati, *And the Violins Stopped Playing* (New York: Franklin Watts, 1986).

16. See Donald Kenrick and Grattan Puxon, *The Destiny of Europe's Gypsies* (London: Chatto Heinemann, 1972), 141. There are apparently only six hundred Gypsies living in Berlin. In the Federal Republic of Germany, the few remaining Gypsies are pressing the Bonn government to make restitution to Gypsy survivors of concentration camps.

17. For an up-to-date account of the life of one million Gypsies in the United States, see Marlene Sway, *Gypsy Life in America* (Urbana: University of Illinois, 1988).

18. Interest on housing loans for Gypsies is nonexistent in Hun-

gary. In Czechoslovakia, after World War II, Slovakian Gypsies were resettled in the homes of Sudetenland Germans after their eviction to West Germany. The USSR claims to have assimilated its Gypsies, but this is problematic. Gypsies are still considered to be an ethnic group in population statistics for the USSR and Yugoslavia, in contrast to other Eastern European countries. A separate Gypsy Theater, formerly the Jewish Theater, thrives in Moscow, and there are official Gypsy cultural exchanges with Hungary. Still the USSR refused to send representatives to World Gypsy Conferences held in the West. Romanian and Bulgarian Gypsies are not completely settled and can be seen traveling in groups with their horses and buggies. The Bulgarian government has ceased to count Gypsies as a minority, although a small Gypsy ghetto exists in the heart of Sofia near the new Rodina Hotel.

19. The Hungarian government maintains that Gypsies constitute only 3.5 percent of the population since Gypsies that "pass" as non-Gypsies are excluded.

20. Draftees had been required to complete eight years of elementary school education before being eligible. Gypsy males frequently dropped out before completion of their eight years and were therefore ineligible for the draft. After 1979, the eight-year school requirement was relaxed to permit the greater drafting of Gypsies.

21. The music of Gypsies influenced many composers of classical music, but especially Liszt. Later composers such as Kodaly and Bartok, while inspired by Hungarian folk music, distinguished between urban Gypsy music, which they held to be inferior, and the "superior" folk music of the Hungarian peasants. For a detailed Soviet study of Hungarian and Gypsy music, see Leksa Manush, "The Problem of the Folk Music of Gypsies," *The Soviet Review* (Summer 1987), 48–65.

22. A much higher percentage of children are now surviving childbirth since 90 to 95 percent of all Gypsies are born in hospitals. See Laszlo Siklos's article on Gypsies in *New Hungarian Quarterly* 40 (Winter 1970), 150–62. I also had the pleasure of visiting a predominantly Gypsy orphanage in Sata in the fall of 1985, which was most impressive.

23. There are still restrictions on the photographing of Gypsy ghettos in Hungary, as this writer can attest from personal experience.

Chapter 8

1. On the average, there was no improvement in the relative income of women in the 1960s. This may be attributable to the downward bias produced by the entry into the labor market of large numbers of former housewives with poor skills and education who were encouraged to work outside the home by the women's movement. See *Economic Report of the President*, 1987, 222.

2. In his Godkin lectures at Harvard in April 1985, Senator Daniel Patrick Moynihan notes that one-third of all children born in 1980 will be dependent on welfare at some time before they become adults. From 1962 to 1982, the fraction of black children under the age of three living with only one parent rose from 30 to 60 percent; for whites, the increase was from 7 to 15 percent. Sylvia Hewlett, *A Lesser Life*, 402, also concludes that "most women are in worse shape than their mothers were." The gap between women who are better off and those at the bottom of the employment hierarchy has also grown in Great Britain in the 1980s. See Elizabeth Wilson, "Thatcherism and Women: After Seven Years," in: Ralph Miliband et al., *Socialist Register*, 206. This is also the general conclusion of William Julius Wilson, *The Truly Disadvantaged* (Chicago: University of Chicago Press, 1987).

3. See United States Department of Commerce, "Income Summary Measures of Families, Unrelated Individuals, and Persons, 1947 to 1979," Washington, D.C., 46. The Gini coefficient is a measure of the deviation of the income distribution from complete equality. It is the area between the diagonal representing the complete equality of the income distribution and the Lorenz curve as a percentage of the entire area of the triangle. A Gini of 0 equals complete equality, and a Gini of 1 represents complete inequality. In 1970, the Gini coefficient for blacks (on a regional basis) was lower (signifying more equality) than white Ginis, according to Sharon Oster, "Are Black Incomes More Equally Distributed?" *American Economist* (Autumn 1970). See also William Stevens, "Philadelphia Blacks: More Get to the Top, But Most Are Low On The Ladder," *The New York Times*, 2 March 1986, 50. The median black income in 1980 was 37 percent less than that of the city's population as a whole; this figure was 32 percent in 1970. At the same time, the portion of the black population earning $35,000 (1983 dollars) from 1967 to 1983 rose from 5.9 to 11.1 percent.

4. Gunnar Myrdal, who favored genuine full employment, came out against affirmative action in the *Atlanta Constitution*, 3 and 6 November 1970 and in *The New York Times*, 13 December 1964, 28.

5. In the postwar years, Paul Samuelson attempted to devise a so-called "neoclassical synthesis," integrating the Keynesian macroeconomic system of ideas and the pre-Keynesian microeconomic paradigm. Alas, the trade-off between the two types of unemployment (overt and covert) represents a disintegration of this attempted synthesis. In effect, we have been practicing employment-creation at the macroeconomic level and employment-saving at the microeconomic level. The need for integration of our macroeconomic and microeconomic theory has been recognized by Axel Leijonhufvud.

6. See Samuel Bowles and Herbert Gintis, *Democracy and Capitalism* (New York: Basic Books, 1986), 82. Also Michael Reich, *Racial Inequality and Class Conflict* (Princeton: Princeton University Press, 1980). See also Howard Sherman, *Radical Political Economy* (Armonk, NY: M.E. Sharpe, 1987), 120.

7. See Bettina Berch, "The Resurrection of Out-Work," *Monthly Review*, November 1985, 37–41.

8. In the words of the *Economic Report of the President*, 1985, 49, "reducing inflation and in time achieving full price stability—zero inflation—is a major goal of this administration."

9. According to the *Economic Report of the President*, 1987, the growth of unit labor costs in the 1980s was 5 percent higher abroad than it was in the United States. IMF estimates for 1987 put unit labor costs in United States manufacturing below their level in 1980. See *Economic Report of the President*, 1988, 115.

10. The use of a different base year (1980) indicates that the age-adjusted rates under Carter remain considerably lower than the Reagan rates. See Robert Horn, "An Age-Adjusted Unemployment Rate," *Challenge*, July-August 1988, 57. See also Richard S. Krashevski, "What is Full Employment?" *Challenge*, November-December 1985, 34, for an alternative calculation using 1965, rather than 1956, as the "normal" labor force weighting year. By mid-1986, the age-adjusted and actual unemployment rates had converged. His conclusion is that if full employment was defined as 4 percent unemployment in 1965, it could also be the target for 1986. Also see my letter to *The New York Times*, 26 February 1986, A-22.

11. The most recent contract of the United Automobile Workers

was settled with only a 2 to 3 percent annual increase in money wages in the interest of job security.

12. The Bay Area Plan called for Bay Area Rapid Transport (BART) to enforce the affirmative action program, but BART failed to do so. Significant minority entrance into local building trades did not take place, and the plan was considered a failure. See Citizens' Commission on Civil Rights, *Affirmative Action*, 43.

13. This phenomenon can also be observed in Great Britain where Britain's entry into the EEC occurred in 1973 despite a majority opinion opposed to this development.

14. Anyone doubting the continued popularity of racism in the United States in 1985 need but look at public reaction to the vigilante activities of Bernhard H. Goetz in New York City and the subsequent waffling of Mayor Koch. According to a Media-Associated Press poll conducted twenty-five years after Martin Luther King's dream of racial equality, 55 percent of the respondents said American society is racist overall, while 37 percent said it is not racist. See *San Jose Mercury News*, 8 August 1988, A-5.

15. If a provision is added for "no rigid quotas," the support for affirmative action has apparently grown in the mid-1980s. See Thomas Ferguson and Joel Rogers, *Right Turn: The Decline of the Democrats and the Future of American Politics* (New York: Hill and Wang, 1986), p. 17. Nevertheless, the Gallup Poll (April 10–13, 1987) measuring the public response to *Johnson v. Santa Clara County Transportation Agency* continues to draw disagreement by more than a two to one ratio with the Supreme Court decision. Blacks favored the decision, and Hispanics were evenly divided. Less than one-third of all women approved, despite the fact that the decision involved Ms. Diane Joyce, who became a road dispatcher despite the fact that her score was slightly lower than that of Paul E. Johnson. See *San Jose Mercury News*, 14 June 1987, C-3.

16. The one possible exception to this generalization is the potential treatment of homosexuals in the armed services since the recent adoption of Section 15 of Canada's relatively new constitution. It also seems clear that Hungary, which has legalized homosexuality, is less discriminatory than the USSR. In January 1988, the Hungarian government permitted the formation of a legal association of gay people to provide AIDS education. See Bruce Shenitz, "Hungary Seeks Its Own Glasnost," *The Nation*, 9 April 1988, 496. This may be partly a reflection of the stage of development since homosexuality is also legal in the GDR, Czechoslovakia, and Poland. Even within

GDR, there seems to be a liberalization over time. In a 1984 interview, Kurt R. Bach, an East German sexologist, affirms that "homosexuals are and remain *precious* [my emphasis] members of the collective. They are colleagues and friends like all the others." Ten years earlier, he had referred to homosexuality as a defect. See Rudiger Preper, "Official Policy and the Attitudes of the GDR Youth Towards the Opposite Sex as Reflected in the Column 'Unter Vier Augen,' " in: *Studies in GDR Culture and Society* 6 (New York: Lanham, 1986), 118. A recent propaganda booklet states: "Homosexual relations are perfectly legal in the GDR. There is no discrimination against homosexuals in either their personal lives or at work. Progress has been made over the past few years in the social acceptance of homosexuals. This is the result of a broad campaign in the mass media and of the growing self-confidence of homosexuals themselves." See *Young People in the GDR* (Berlin: Panorama DDR, 1987), 48. The USSR, which is still composed of the comparatively underdeveloped, agricultural republics in Central Asia, is therefore less advanced in its treatment of gays, as explained above. In pronatalist and less developed Romania, homosexuality is also illegal, possibly as a reflection of the country's lower level of economic development and the higher percentage of its population still found in agriculture. China is an obvious candidate for the legalization and encouragement of homosexuality as an antidote to the growth of female infanticide in the era of the one-child family. In this manner, the future gender imbalance might tend to be offset by the growth of male homosexuality and penalties for lesbians. For statistics on the lopsided ratio of boys to girls in China, see Vern L. Bullough and Fang-Fu Ruan, "China's Children," *The Nation*, 18 June 1988, 848–49.

17. The virtual disappearance of support for the labor theory of value, the admission of the existence of a market for labor power, the resurrection of theories of genetic superiority (including the possibility of sperm banks), the development of a stock market, and the acceptance of the surveillance of the International Monetary Fund are good examples of this revisionism.

18. The attraction of intelligent, risk-preferring people to the market and risk-avoiding individuals to the state or government, seems obvious under actually existing capitalism, and can also been seen by studying migration from socialist to nonsocialist market countries.

19. The mushrooming of tanning salons (solariums) and make-up

parlors ("Kozmetika") in private apartments are obvious examples of this phenomenon.

20. The proportion of Gypsies in Hungary is the highest in the world, according to Laszlo Siklos, in *New Hungarian Quarterly* 40 (Winter 1970). "The relations between Gypsies and the general population in other countries are not as difficult and contradictory as in Hungary. The Gypsies are only one of the many nationalities living in the Soviet Union. There is no discrimination against them."

21. In the fall of 1985, I spent my sabbatical studying the Hungarian Gypsy problem, which included traveling to the Northeast of Hungary as a guest of Dr. Kozak Istvanne, the government's specialist in Hungarian Gypsy affairs. I also had an opportunity to visit Michael Stewart, a young British doctoral candidate in anthropology who was living in a Gypsy ghetto near Gyongos. Many of the above materials and conclusions on the status of Hungarian Gypsies came from these two experiences, and the author is grateful to both for their time and efforts on his behalf. Generally speaking, those Hungarians who had grown up having contact with Gypsies had a more positive attitude toward the potential of the depressed Gypsy population.

22. Fred Weir, *Canadian Tribune*, 2 May 1988, argues that "the USSR is in the grip of what can only be described as a new social revolution—'perestroika.' For Soviet women, over the past two years perhaps the most important development has been the creation of a mass women's movement, the women's councils, which now exist in virtually every workplace and community." The Gorbachev anti-alcohol campaign is also extremely popular with Soviet women. The 27th Party Congress was the first during which the nonwhite Republics of Central Asia were singled out for criticism. My informants in Moscow claim that this criticism was cleared with minority experts before the Party Congress. Where ethnic cliques and nepotism have interfered with greater efficiency, there is clearly a contradiction in Soviet policy with respect to minorities in the Gorbachev era. There is also a contradiction between affirmative action and integration in general, as pointed out by Rasma Karlins, *Ethnic Relations in the USSR* (London: Allen and Unwin, 1986), 94–95. In the United States, this same contradiction shows up in the positions of integrated blacks and the need for continued affirmative action. The positions of black conservatives such as Thomas Sowell, Glenn C. Loury, and Clarence Pendleton, Jr. reflect this contradiction. It

can also be found in the positions of successful, integrated black non-conservatives such as Charles Hamilton and Harry Edwards.

23. *Soviet News*, 2 December 1987, 432. See also Mikhail Gorbachev, *Perestroika* (New York: Harper and Row, 1987), 116–18.

24. This conclusion is reinforced by responses from a small sample of women who have lived in both countries for extended periods of time.

25. Victor Perlo also emphasizes the failure of affirmative action, particularly in the Reagan years. He praises trade unions for leading "important campaigns to win serious affirmative action gains, including use of specific goals and *quotas* [my emphasis] to provide for decisive advances." His interpretation of the role of the Cold War is thus rather different from mine. "What has it [the Cold War] cost the United States? A generation's loss of hard-won labor and civil rights gains." Victor Perlo, *Super Profits and Crises: Modern U.S. Capitalism* (New York: International Publishers, 1988), 107, 503.

26. See Peter Temin, *Did Monetary Forces Cause the Great Depression?* (New York: W. W. Norton, 1976). It should be noted that Temin specifically rejects the "underconsumptionist" implications of his research showing a sharp decline in consumption in 1930. It is traditional for both mainstream and Marxist theoreticians to reject underconsumptionist conclusions.

27. See David Colander, "Was Keynes a Keynesian or a Lernerian?" *Journal of Economic Literature* (December 1984), 1572–75, for an interesting account of Keynes's first reaction to "functional finance" and his later acceptance of this principle as a natural offspring of his *General Theory*. Functional finance assumes that federal taxation is unnecessary for revenue purposes since monetization of the debt—printing and selling Treasury bonds to the Fed—is a suitable alternative.

28. By 1948, eight million Germans were expelled from areas incorporated into postwar Poland, Czechoslovakia, and the Soviet zone of Germany. They flooded the labor market of the western zones of Germany. Six million refugees from Japan's former Asian empire had also been repatriated. See Philip Armstrong et al., *Capitalism Since World War II* (London: Fontana Paperback, 1984), 25–26. This volume presents considerable evidence for a falling rate of profit after 1966 in the advanced capitalist system. The authors tend to downplay the destruction of manufacturing capital, but the loss of transportation and social capital (housing) remains significant.

29. A recent study commissioned by the United States Navy found that major military contractors made twice as much profit selling weapons to the Pentagon as they did selling manufactured products elsewhere during the Carter years. By 1983, profits were 3.3 times higher. See *Dollars and Sense*, July-August 1987, 4.

30. See Peter Hooper, "The Dollar, External Imbalance, and the United States Economy," a paper presented at the Western Economic Association meetings in Vancouver, B.C., July 1987. The index of the CPI adjusted exchange rate of the dollar shows that for G-10 and eight UDCs combined, the 1986 index was still above the value of the dollar in March 1973. In 1986, the United States received income of $88 billion on assets owned abroad, while it paid out $67 billion on foreign-owned assets in the United States. Therefore, in terms of income received and paid, the United States was a net creditor in 1986. See *Economic Report of the President*, 1988, 98–99.

31. Walt Rostow, *Getting From Here To There* (New York: McGraw-Hill, 1978), 51.

32. Richard A. Easterlin, *Birth and Fortune* (New York: Basic Books, 1987), 156. Easterlin expected fertility rates to be well above replacement levels by the mid-1990s.

33. For an early recognition of this need for bold fiscal policy by Gunnar Myrdal, see a report of Werner Wiskari, "Myrdal Terms U.S. Stagnant: Wages Wide Economic Reform," *The New York Times*, 22 July 1962, 38. Most public opinion polls in both Great Britain and the United States show that the public favors both tax cuts and an expanded welfare state. Even leftist analysis assumes there is something illogical about such a policy. See Elizabeth Wilson, *Socialist Register*, 218.

34. For an early appreciation of the counterproductive role of real interest in the advanced capitalist system, see Roy F. Harrod, *Towards a Dynamic Economics* (London: Macmillan and Co., 1948), 159. See also my *The Contrasting Economies* (Boston: Allyn and Bacon, 1963), 207–208. Similar thinking underlies Robert Eisner, *How Real Is The Federal Deficit?* (New York: The Free Press, 1986).

35. See Peter Hooper, cited in note 30.

Glossary

Absolute poverty.   The condition of persons living below the poverty line in the United States.

Accelerated depreciation.   Tax incentive granted to corporate enterprises in advanced capitalist system enabling them to write off depreciation costs at a rapid rate, thereby reducing current taxes and stimulating or subsidizing investment.

Acceleration principle.   The tendency, under certain circumstances, for changes in the consumption and output of consumers' goods to stimulate much greater proportional changes in investment and in the output or inventories of producers' goods.

Active deficit.   Budget deficit at full employment. Also referred to as "structural deficit."

Actually existing socialism.   Term coined by Rudolf Bahro to describe conditions in Eastern Europe. By the same token, we can use "actually existing capitalism" to describe advanced Western economies.

Administered price policy.   Rigidity to price changes on the downside by monopolistic enterprises and/or unions which has retarded the decline in price and wage levels in the United States despite the growth of underutilized capital and labor resources, especially the former. Also referred to as "sticky" pricing.

Asymmetrical fiscal policy. A policy of continually stimulating the advanced capitalist economy through increased government expenditures, cutting of tax rates, or subsidization of the investment and consumption processes, all the time with comparative disregard for inflationary pressures.

Balanced equivalents. Maoist term to justify balance of exports and imports, lack of borrowing from abroad, and minimal role of foreign trade.

Buyers' market. Sellers searching for scarce buyers. Characteristic of advanced capitalist system in peacetime with problems of inadequate and slowly growing effective demand relative to rapidly growing productive capabilities.

Cost-push inflation. Increase in price levels attributed to wages rising faster than labor productivity and resulting in rising unit labor costs. See also supply-side inflation.

Covert unemployment. Poor utilization of labor and capital in make-work or wasteful activities.

Crowding in. Tendency for disguised saving to appear in FL economy as underutilized resources become employed again.

Crowding out. Tendency for government spending to use resources that supposedly might be used by private sector in NFL economy.

Demand-pull inflation. Increases in the price level resulting from excessive demand relative to available supplies.

Disguised unemployment.   See covert unemployment.

Disproportionality.   Tendency for investment to outpace consumption possibilities. See also proportionality.

Employment-creating institutions.   Any measure which tends to have as its principal purpose the creation of jobs, rather than utility or satisfaction. Advanced capitalist institutions such as redundant advertising, foreign aid, military and space expenditures.

Employment-saving institutions.   Any measure which has as its principal purpose the reduction of jobs. The elimination of redundant administrative jobs, the introduction of automated equipment, and the welcoming of an import surplus might be included.

Exchange rate mercantilism.   A country's deliberate weakening of its currency in order to export unemployment and obtain economic growth. Applicable to Canadian policy in 1961, Nixon's New Economic Policy in 1971, and Reagan's Plaza Hotel agreement in 1985.

Export-Import Bank.   A public corporation created by an executive order of President Roosevelt in February 1934. It makes or guarantees low-cost loans to encourage exports.

Extensive stage of development.   The early stage of capitalist or noncapitalist development when the mobilization of underutilized resources may be a principal source of growth.

Fiscal policy.   The use of government revenue, expenditures, and general budgetary policies to achieve desired economic objectives. An easy fiscal policy is characterized by active deficits, while a tight fiscal policy would be indicated by a budget surplus.

Free lunch (FL).   Economies that operate within their production possibilities curve need not make a choice between two allocations of resources. They can have their cake and eat it too.

Functional finance.   The assumption that federal taxation is unnecessary for revenue purposes since federal spending can be financed by monetizing the debt, that is, printing Treasury bonds to be purchased by the Fed.

Intensive stage of development.   The stage following the extensive one, when greater attention must be paid to the more efficient allocation of scarce resources as a source of growth.

Investment tax credit.   Linking of investment to forgiveness of corporate profits tax beginning in 1962. Suspended briefly in 1966 and again under Nixon until August 15, 1971. Eliminated in tax reform of 1986.

Labor force participation rate.   The percentage of the population, or the normal working age group in a population, taking part in production.

Labor productivity.   Output per unit of labor input. Changes in productivity result from changes in the technical skills of workers and/or increases in the mechanization of the productive process.

Law of value.   A Marxist concept describing the functioning of the free market forces in a capitalist-oriented economy. As a result of this law, there is supposedly a tendency for products to be exchanged at prices that reflect their labor content, both living and "stored-up."

Macroeconomics.   The study of economic aggregates of public and private consumption and investment and their impact on the economy's level of employment, incomes, and prices. The study of how the economy answers the basic question, "How much will be produced?"

Microeconomics.   The study of market pricing and output decisions in such individual units as the firm or industry. The study of how the economy answers the questions, "What is produced? How is it produced? For whom is it produced?"

Mini-recession.   A period of about one year—from mid-1966 to mid-1967—when the United States economy failed to grow significantly, despite the rapid escalation of Vietnam expenditures. A capacity hangover following an investment binge. In the Federal Republic of Germany, this period was characterized by an actual decline in industrial production, the first experience of this type since World War II.

Monetary policy.   The management of a nation's money supply so that credit will be available in the quantity and at a price consistent with desired objectives, such as stemming demand-pull inflation or (less frequently or successfully) stimulating growth. An easy monetary policy would be indicated by low or negative real interest rates, while a tight monetary policy would result in high real interest rates.

New economics.   The name given to the fiscal policy pursued during the Kennedy-Johnson administrations, which resulted in eight years of sustained growth, marred only by the mini-recession of 1966-1967.

No free lunch (NFL).   Economies operating on their production possibilities curve where choice between alternative expenditures becomes relevant.

Overt unemployment.   Officially recorded rate of unemployment.

Passive deficit. Budget deficit caused mainly by the falloff of revenues in recessions and periods of persistent stagnation when unemployed resources cannot pay taxes.

Progressive taxes. Taxes that tend to redistribute income from the rich to the poor.

Proportionality. The relationship between the relative importance of consumption and investment as components of gross national product.

Public Law 480. Legislation providing for the "sale" of United States agricultural surpluses for inconvertible local currencies in an attempt to disguise the grants involved.

Realization problem. The realization problem asks the question: Is there sufficient monetary demand for the commodities which have been produced to be sold, and sold at their value? It was a preoccupation of classical economists, especially Karl Marx.

Real interest rate. Money interest rate deflated (or inflated) by the rate of inflation (or deflation).

Regressive taxation. Taxation that hits lower income groups harder than upper income groups.

Relative poverty. After dividing a nation's distribution of family incomes into quartiles, those families living in the lowest quartile are defined as living in relative poverty.

Reserve army. Marxist term describing chronic existence of unemployed labor in capitalist economies.

Say's Law. The French economist J. B. Say (1767-1832) is credited with formulating the "law" that production creates its own demand. As a result, there can never be a chronic glut or overproduction resulting from deficient demand, as argued originally by Malthus. This law was discredited for the advanced capitalist countries by Lord Keynes, but is still applicable in noncapitalist and developing countries.

Secular stagnation. A long period characterized by the growing inadequacy of investment-like activities to utilize fully the resources released by voluntary nonconsumption at full employment.

Sellers' market. Buyers searching for scarce products or labor. A characteristic of noncapitalist economies and wartime capitalist economies with chronic conditions of inadequate supply relative to effective demand.

Structural deficit. The federal deficit remaining after full employment is achieved and the passive deficit eliminated.

Stumpage fees. Depletion charges levied on the exploitation of easily accessible timber reserves.

Supply-side economics. An attempt to revert to the economics of the nineteenth century with the assumption that Say's Law works in the advanced capitalist system. General approach of the Reagan administration when Keynesian demand management was thought to be in crisis. Ardent supply-siders never worry about the deficit; they argue that there can never be enough investment and believe that a resurrection of the gold standard is called for since it worked so well in the nineteenth century. President Reagan accepted a tight monetary policy to control inflation, but ardent supply-siders (Representative Jack Kemp, for example) rejected this concession to conventional wisdom.

Supply-side inflation. Inflation coming from underutilization of both labor and capital and from rising unit overhead costs. It may also describe inflation as a result of tax increases (including the excise tax imposed on the United States economy by OPEC in 1973), expenditures on cleaning up the environment, and rising real interest rates, as in the 1980s. It does not come from wage increases since larger wage increases are necessary to get back to demand-pull inflation. At that point, and only then, control of wage increases by an incomes policy becomes relevant.

Swing credit.   The practice in trade between the Federal Republic of Germany and the German Democratic Republic whereby the West German export surplus is considered as an interest free "loan" to the GDR.

Symmetrical fiscal policy.   The orthodox post-Keynesian view that there are twin problems: inflation and deflation, and that fiscal policy must alternate between contraction and expansion. The achievement of full employment without significant inflation is simply a "fine-tuning" problem.

Tight money policy.   A policy of the Federal Reserve System to reduce the amount of excess reserves held by member banks, and thereby discouraging loans and investments by banks, making credit more difficult to obtain, and restraining growth in the money supply.

Velocity of money.   The average turnover of the monetary stock per year. It was rising by 3 percent per annum until 1981, after which it actually declined for a number of years, as an indication of the underlying weakness of the economy and the impossibility of "pushing on a string."

Weighting problem.   This problem arises as a result of changes in the structure of what is being measured over time. For example, changes in the structure of the labor force mean that crude unemployment rates must be age-adjusted. Changes in the regional structure of infants born might require that crude infant mortality rates be adjusted to reflect the regional structure in a certain base year. Price indexes depend on the market basket used. An early year structure of consumption will produce an upward bias in the Consumer Price Index since no account is taken of substitution effects.

Bibliography

Adam, Jan. *Employment and Wage Policies in Poland, Czechoslovakia and Hungary Since 1950*. New York: St. Martin's Press, 1984.

Alexeyeva, Ludmilla. *Soviet Dissent*. Middletown, CT: Wesleyan University Press, 1987.

Allen, Robert L. *Black Awakening in Capitalist America* Garden City: Doubleday, 1969.

———. *Reluctant Reformers: Racism and Social Reform Movements in the United States*. Washington, D.C.: Howard University Press, 1984.

Anderson, Martin. *Revolution*. New York: Harcourt Brace Jovanovich, 1988.

Angell, Norman. *The Great Illusion: A Study of the Relations of Military Power to National Advantage*. London: G. P. Putnam's Sons, 1914.

Aptheker, Herbert, ed. *Newspaper Columns of W. E. B. DuBois*. White Plains, NY: Kraus-Thomson, White Plains, 1986.

Armstrong, Philip, et al. *Capitalism Since World War II*. London: Fontana, 1984.

Baldwin, James. *The Fire Next Time*. New York: Dell, 1962.

Baran, Paul, and Paul Sweezy. *Monopoly Capital*. New York: Monthly Review Press, 1966.

Becker, Gary. *The Economics of Discrimination*. Chicago: University of Chicago Press, 1957.

Berch, Bettina. *The Endless Day*. New York: Harcourt Brace Jovanovich, 1982.

Bernard, Philippe J. *Planning in the Soviet Union*. Oxford: Pergamon Press, 1966.

Berlowitz, Marvin J., and Carol E. Morgan. *Racism, Imperialism, and Peace*. Minneapolis: MEP Publications, 1987.

Block, Walter, and Michael A. Walker. *On Employment Equity*. Vancouver, B.C.: The Fraser Institute, 1985.

Bogart, Leo, ed. *Social Research and the Desegregation of the U.S. Army*. Chicago: Markham Publishing, 1969.

Bowles, Samuel. *Beyond the Wasteland*. Garden City: Doubleday, 1983.

Bowles, Samuel, and Richard Edwards. *Understanding Capitalism*. New York: Harper and Row, 1985.

Browning, Genia K. *Women and Politics in the USSR: Consciousness Raising and Soviet Women's Groups*. New York: St. Martin's Press, 1987.

Burkin, Martin, et al. *Blacks and the Military*. Washington, D.C.: The Brookings Institution, 1982.

Carr, Edward Hallett. *The Soviet Impact on the Western World*. New York: Macmillan, 1947.

Citizens' Commission on Civil Rights. *Affirmative Action to Open the Doors of Job Opportunity: A Policy of Fairness and Compassion that Has Worked*. Washington, D.C., 1984.

Cockburn, Alexander. *Corruptions of Empire*. New York: Verso, 1987.

Commission on Minority Participation in Education and American Life. *One-Third of a Nation*. Washington, D.C.: American Council on Education, 1988.

Congdon, Tim. *The Debt Threat*. New York: Basil Blackwell, 1988.

Conquest, Robert, ed. *The Last Empire: Nationality and the Soviet Future*. Stanford: Hoover University Press, 1986.

Council of Economic Advisers. *Economic Report of the President*, 1985-1988. Washington, D.C.: Government Printing Office.

Cripps, Thomas. *Black Film as Genre*. Bloomington: Indiana University, 1979.

De Bardeleben, Joan. *Environment and Marxism-Leninism: The Soviet and East German Experience*. Boulder: Westview Press, 1985.

De Grasse, Robert W., Jr. *Military Expansion, Economic Decline*. Armonk, NY: M. E. Sharpe, 1983.

Dowd, Douglas. *The Waste of Nations*. Boulder: Westview Press, 1989.

Draper, Theodore. *American Communism and Soviet Russia*. New York: Octagon, 1977.

Easterlin, Richard A. *Birth and Fortune*. New York: Basic Books, 1987.

Economic Commission for Europe. *The Economic Role of Women in the ECE Region, Developments, 1975/85*. New York: United Nations, 1985.

Edwards, John. *Positive Discrimination, Social Justice, and Social Policy: Moral Scrutiny of a Policy Practice*. London: Tavistock, 1987.

Eisner, Robert. *How Real Is the Federal Deficit?* New York: The Free Press, 1986.

Ellman, Michael. *Collectivization, Convergence and Capitalism: Political Economy in a Divided World*. London: Academic Press, 1984.

Farley, Jennie, ed. *Women Workers in 15 Countries*. Ithaca, NY: ILR Press, 1985.

Ferguson, Thomas, and Joel Rogers. *Right Turn: The Decline of the Democrats and the Future of American Politics*. New York: Hill and Wang, 1986.

Foner, Eric. *Reconstruction—Politics and Government—1865-1977*. New York: Harper and Row, 1988.

Foner, Jack D. *Blacks and the Military in American History: A New Perspective*. New York: Praeger, 1974.

Foster, William Z. *The Negro People in America*. New York: International Publishers, 1954.

Gervasi, Tom. *The Myth of Soviet Military Supremacy*. New York: Harper and Row, 1986.

Gorbachev, Mikhail. *Perestroika*. New York: Harper and Row, 1987.

Greider, William. *Secrets of the Temple: How the Federal Reserve Runs the Country*. New York: Simon and Schuster, 1987.

Gruliow, Leo. *Soviet Views in the Postwar World Economy: An Official Critique of Eugene Varga's "Changes in the Economy of Capitalism Resulting from the Second World War."* Washington, D.C.: Public Affairs Press, 1948.

Harrison, Mark. *Soviet Planning in Peace and War.* Cambridge: Cambridge University Press, 1986.

Harrod, Roy F. *Towards a Dynamic Economics*. London: Macmillan and Co., 1948.

Hewlett, Sylvia. *A Lesser Life: The Myth of Women's Liberation in America*. New York: William Morrow, 1986.

Holland, Barbara, ed. *Soviet Sisterhood*. Bloomington: Indiana

University Press, 1985.

Horvath, Branko. *The Political Economy of Socialism*. Armonk, NY: M. E. Sharpe, 1982.

Ivanov, Robert. *Blacks in United States History*. Moscow: Progress, 1985.

Janeway, Eliot. *The Economics of Crisis, War, Politics and the Dollar*. New York: Weybright and Talley, 1968.

Jones, H. James. *Bad Blood*. London: Allen and Unwin, 1986.

Kamerman, Sheila B., and Alfred J. Kahn. *Child Care, Family Benefits, and Working Parents*. New York: Columbia University Press, 1981.

Kenrick, Donald, and Grattan Puxon. *The Destiny of Europe's Gypsies*. London: Chatto Heinemann, 1972.

Keynes, John Maynard. *The General Theory of Employment, Interest and Money*. New York: Harcourt, Brace and World, 1936.

Keyssar, Alexander. *The First Century of Unemployment in Massachusetts*. New York: Cambridge University Press, 1986.

Kirby, John B. *Black Americans in the Roosevelt Era*. Knoxville: University of Tennessee Press, 1980.

Kome, Penney. *Women of Influence: Canadian Women and Politics*. Garden City: Doubleday, 1985.

Lane, David. *The End of Equality*. London: Penguin Books, 1971.

Laslett, John H. M., and Seymour Martin Lipset, eds. *Failure of a Dream?* Berkeley: University of California Press, 1974.

Leahy, Margaret E. *Development Strategies and the Status of Women*. Boulder: Lynne Rienner, 1986.

Lewis, W. Arthur. *Racial Conflict and Economic Development*. Cambridge: Harvard University Press, 1985.

Lorimer, Frank. *The Population of the Soviet Union: History and Prospects*. Geneva: League of Nations, 1946.

Lunarduri, Christine A. *From Equal Suffrage to Equal Rights*. New York: New York University Press, 1986.

MacDougall, Curtis D. *Gideon's Army*. New York: Marzani and Munsell, 1965.

Mandel, William. *Soviet But Not Russian*. Edmonton, Canada: University of Alberta Press, 1985.

Mamonova, Tatyana, ed. *Women and Russia*. Boston: Beacon Press, 1984.

Mathews, Mervyn. *Education in the Soviet Union*. Boston: Allen and Unwin, 1982.

Medvedev, Zhores. *Andropov*. New York: W. W. Norton, 1983.

Miliband, Ralph. *Socialist Register*. London: The Merlin Press, 1987.

Moses, Joel C. *The Politics of Women and Work in the Soviet Union and the United States*. Berkeley: Institute of International Studies, 1983.

Myrdal, Gunnar. *An American Dilemma*. New York: Harper and Row, 1962.

Nalty, Bernard C. *Strength for the Fight: A History of Black Americans in the Military*. New York: The Free Press, 1986.

Nichols, Leo. *Breakthrough on the Color Front*. New York: Random House, 1953.

Nove, Alec, and J. A. Newth. *The Soviet Middle East: A Communist Model for Development*. London: Frederick A. Praeger, 1967.

Oren, Dan A. *Joining the Club*. New Haven: Yale University Press, 1986.

Parsons, Howard L. *Christianity Today in the USSR*. New York: International Publishers, 1987.

Perlo, Victor. *Super Profits and Crises: Modern U.S. Capitalism*. New York: International Publishers, 1988.

Ramati, Alexander. *And the Violins Stopped Playing*. New York: Franklin Watts, 1986.

Reich, Michael. *Racial Inequality and Class Conflict*. Princeton: Princeton University Press, 1980.

Report of the Commission on Equality in Employment. Ottawa: 1984.

Ross, Arthur M., and Herbert Hill. *Employment, Race and Poverty*. New York: Harcourt, Brace and World, 1967.

Rostow, Walt. *Getting From Here To There*. New York: McGraw-Hill, 1978.

Scharf, Lois. *To Work and to Wed: Female Employment, Feminism and the Great Depression*. Westport, CT: Greenwood Press, 1980.

Schiller, Bradley R. *The Economics of Poverty and Discrimination*. 4th ed. Englewood Cliffs, NJ: Prentice-Hall, 1984.

Shaffer, Harry. *Women in the Two Germanies: A Comparative Study of a Socialist and a Non-Socialist Society*. New York: Pergamon Press, 1981.

Shaffer, Harry G., ed. *The Soviet System in Theory and Practice*. 2nd ed. New York: Frederick Ungar, 1984.

Sherman, Howard, *Radical Political Economy*. Armonk, NY: M. E. Sharpe, 1987.

Sitkoff, Harvard. *A New Deal for Blacks: The Emergence of Civil*

Rights as a National Issue. New York: Oxford, 1978.

Sommers, Albert T. *The U.S. Economy Demystified.* Lexington, MA: Lexington Books, 1985.

Southern, David W. *Gunnar Myrdal and Black-White Relations: The Use and Abuse of An American Dilemma, 1944-1969.* Baton Rouge: Louisiana State University Press, 1987.

Sowell, Thomas. *Markets and Minorities.* New York: Basic Books, 1981.

Steakley, James D. *The Homosexual Emancipation Movement in Germany.* New York: Arno Press, 1975.

Sway, Marlene. *Gypsy Life in America.* Urbana: University of Illinois, 1988.

Szymanski, Albert. *Human Rights in the Soviet Union.* London: Zed, 1984.

Temin, Peter. *Did Monetary Forces Cause the Great Depression?* New York: W. W. Norton, 1976.

Tomiak, J. J. *Soviet Education in the 1980s.* London: Croom Helm, 1983.

Turgeon, Lynn. *The Contrasting Economies.* Boston: Allyn and Bacon, 1963. Reprint 1969.

———. *The Advanced Capitalist System.* Armonk, NY: M. E. Sharpe, 1980.

———. *The Economics of Discrimination.* Studies on Developing Countries Monograph # 62. Budapest: Center for Afro-Asian Research of Hungarian Academy of Sciences, 1973.

Wilbur, Charles K. *The Soviet Model and Underdeveloped Countries.* Chapel Hill: University of North Carolina Press, 1969.

Williamson, Joel. *The Crucible of Race: Black-White Relations in the American South Since Emancipation.* New York: Oxford University Press, 1984.

Wilson, William Julius. *The Declining Significance of Race.* Chicago: University of Chicago Press, 1980.

———. *The Truly Disadvantaged.* Chicago: University of Chicago Press, 1987.

Wolfe, Alan. *America's Impasse: The Rise and Fall of the Politics of Growth.* Boston: South End Press, 1981.

Index

Temen, Peter, 143 (n25)
Thatcher, Margaret, 58, 128 (n22)
Third World, 24, 55
Thomas, Norman, 23
Thurmond, Strom, 23
Thurow, Lester, 3
Tipping point, 122 (n4)
Tobin, James, 84
Trade-offs, 85
Trade unions, 18, 33, 139 (n11)
Treasury, Secretary of, 99
Treasury Accord, 17, 110 (n17)
Trost, Cathy, 114 (n3)
Trudeau, Pierre, 55
Truman, Harry, 10, 23–24, 38–39, 42, 102
Turgeon, Lynn, 134 (n40)
Turkmenia, 131 (n23)
Turnover tax, 69
Tuskegee Institute, 32
Tuskegee syphilis experiment, 118 (n28)

Ukraine, 68
Underconsumption, 4–5
Underground economy, 15
Unemployment, 34
Unemployment compensation, 112 (n27)
Unions. *See* trade unions
Unit labor costs, 104
United Automobile Workers (UAW), 139 (n11)
United Farm Workers (UFW), 35
United Kingdom. *See* Great Britain
United Nations, 61
United States Chamber of Commerce, 124 (n15)
United States Commission on Civil Rights, 37, 44
USSR, 24–26, 57, 59–72, 128–134 (n1–44)
Uzbekistan, 61

Value added tax, 99, 105
Varga, Eugene, 9
Varga, Zoltan, 136 (n11)
Versailles Treaty, 9
Vietnam War, 16, 40, 84–85, 97
Volatility, 30
Volcker, Paul, 97, 103
Volga Germans, 63
Volga River Project, 41

Wages, 14
Wallace, Henry, 23–24, 27, 35
War on Poverty, 116 (n11)
Warren, Earl, 40
Washington, George, 30
Weidenbaum, Murray, 102
Weighting problem, 118 (n22)
Weir, Fred, 142 (n22)
Weisskopf, Thomas, 3
Western European, 10
Whip inflation now (WIN), 101
Williamson, Joel, 28
Willkie, Wendell, 25
Wilson, Woodrow, 33
Withholding tax, 16
Women, 29
Works Progress Administration (WPA), 27

Yale University, 123 (n12)
Yalta Agreement, 10
Yugoslavia, 73

About the Author

Lynn Turgeon is Professor of Economics at Hofstra University. Ideas for this book were stimulated by his sabbatical leave in Budapest in 1985, when he studied Gypsies; it reflects his extensive travels in Eastern Europe and the U.S.S.R. and his Fulbright lectureship at Moscow State University in 1978. He is also author of *The Advanced Capitalist System*, published by M. E. Sharpe in 1980.